Promoting Harmony
Young Adolescent Development
and School Practices

Promoting Harmony
Young Adolescent Development
and School Practices

John Van Hoose
David Strahan
Mark L'Esperance

National Middle School Association
Westerville, Ohio

National Middle School Association
4151 Executive Parkway
Suite 300
Westerville, Ohio 43081
Telephone (800) 528-NMSA
www.nmsa.org

Printed in the United States of America.
Third printing March, 2006

Sue Swaim, Executive Director
Jeff Ward, Deputy Executive Director
April Tibbles, Director of Publications
Dawn Williams, Production Specialist
Edward Brazee, Editor, Professional Publications
John Lounsbury, Consulting Editor, Professional Publications
Mary Mitchell, Designer and Editorial Assistant
Mark Shumaker, Graphic Designer
Marcia Meade-Hurst, Senior Publications Representative

Photographs by Tim Vacula
Cover photo by Rod Reilly

Library of Congress Cataloging-in-Publication Data
Van Hoose, John.
    Promoting harmony: young adolescent development and school
practices/John Van Hoose, David Strahan, Mark L'Esperance.
      p. cm.
    Enlarged ed. of: Young adolescent development and school practices. c1988.
    Includes bibliographical references.
    ISBN: 1-56090-170-5 (pbk.)
    1. Middle school students--United States. 2. Adolescence. 3. Middle
schools--United States. I. Strahan, David B. II. L'Esperance, Mark, date-III. Van
Hoose, John. Young adolescent development and school practices. IV. National
Middle School Association. V. Title.

    LB1135.V28 2001
    373.18--dc21   2001031486

Dedication

To my father and my brother, special heroes and role models in my life who have been so giving and loving and civil to so many. Would that all of us could be the role models to our students that they have been to me.

And my profound gratitude to my wife, Dale, my daughter, Sarah, and my son, Matt. No woman could be more loving and more concerned for a person than Dale is for me. No daughter or son could be more supportive and more willing to go out of their way to be of help in times of crises. The world is better off because of these beautiful people. I am so blessed to have the privilege of sharing my life with them.

— John Van Hoose

To our two sons, Andrew and Alex. Their journey through early adolescence has convinced me that our youth are often stronger and wiser than society realizes. The care and nurture they received from teachers and administrators at Jamestown Middle School reaffirmed my conviction that developmentally responsive education is not only possible, but absolutely necessary. Watching these two youngsters become young men confirmed everything I believe about the middle grades.

And to my wife Sandie. Her love for teaching is inspiring and her love for our family makes everything possible.

— Dave Strahan

To my wife Pam and three special children, Nicole, Marie, and Stephen. The Lord truly blessed me with a loving and supportive family.

— Mark L'Esperance

Contents

Foreword
The Heart and Soul of Middle Schools

The premise of this book is deceptively simple – "the process of becoming a successful school begins with an understanding of young adolescents and an appreciation for their unique needs." While this sounds like the thesis of innumerable middle level articles, books, and classroom resources, *Promoting Harmony* delivers the goods. It shows how teachers, students, and parents can work together in harmony – and illustrates occasions when school practices are not in harmony.

This is one reason why the original *Young Adolescent Development and School Practices: Promoting Harmony*, first published in 1988, became one of National Middle School Association's best sellers for nearly 13 years. With chapters on physical, sexual, intellectual, and social development, and one on the personal characteristics of young adolescents, plus a concluding chapter, the book was influential in helping thousands of educators and other adults gain a real understanding of young adolescents.

In similar fashion, this enlarged edition will help to educate new generations of middle level educators, parents, and other adults about young adolescents and the practices that we must put in place for schools to be both academically rigorous and developmentally responsive.

While common sense suggests that middle schools should match the needs of young adolescents with school practices, this is not always the case. Recently the reality of high-stakes testing has had a huge and mostly negative impact on appropriate programs for young adolescents. As the authors point out, "...key middle level concepts such as advisory programs have been abandoned as a direct result of pressure to raise test scores" (p. 3).

Promoting Harmony is essentially a brand new book. Completely updated concepts and resources offer an intimate glimpse into the development of 10-15-year-olds and more importantly, provide insights into what their behavior means. Comments by young adolescents and their teachers give a needed perspective and demonstrate an up-front view of the issues confronting young adolescents.

The authors have done a superb job of searching out current research and best practices for each chapter. It is obvious that they know young adolescents, and they recognize too that we understand their trials and tribulations best when we hear from young adolescents themselves.

This is one of those books that should be read by every teacher and every parent of young adolescents because it provides an understanding of 10-15-year-olds not readily available elsewhere. Further, the many discussions of harmonious school practices make this publication a gold mine of ideas that can be used to make schools better places for young adolescents.

Special thanks to David Strahan, Mark L'Esperance, and the late John Van Hoose for their conscientious efforts to provide this essential resource. John Van Hoose, one of the nation's leading authorities in middle level education, fulfilled his leadership role in developing this revision just prior to his death in 2001. John Van Hoose, a longtime professor at the University of North Carolina at Greensboro where he established the Middle Grades Teacher Education Program, was an active leader in the North Carolina Middle School Association, and the National Middle School Association. John's vitality and commitment to young people inspired all who knew him, and he will be sorely missed. As did its predecessor, this book will significantly and positively impact the way educators, parents, and the community view young adolescents.

Edward N. Brazee
Editor

Preface

Our contributions to this publication were enhanced by innumerable contacts with students, teachers, and administrators in the university's professional development schools, Guilford and Jamestown Middle Schools in the Guilford County Public Schools, Greensboro, North Carolina. The vignettes were provided by our students in the University of North Carolina at Greensboro's Middle Grades Program. One author also learned much from participating in the exemplary middle school partnership initiated by Champion International Paper Corporation. Many students, heroes without any role models except at school, taught us so much. The authors of the original version of this work were assisted in the revision by Mark L'Esperance of the University of East Carolina. His knowledge of research and his perspective added substantially to this work.

We have been fortunate to have countless teachers and administrators as role models, educators who cared for, worked for, and loved students. We hope that we will continue to be as effective as they have been in reaching out to needy, challenged young people during what, for them, is the most fragile time of life.

— *The Authors*

Introduction

> Nothing is real with us. You know, sometimes I'll
> catch myself talking to a girl friend, and realize I
> don't mean half of what I'm saying. I don't really
> think a beer blast on the river bottom is supercool,
> but I'll rave about one to a girl friend just to be
> saying something. She smiled at me. "I never told
> anyone that. I think you're the first person I've ever
> really gotten through to." It seems like we're always
> searching for something to satisfy us, and never
> finding it.
>
> —Cherry to Ponyboy
> in *The Outsiders* (Hinton, 1967)

One of the reasons for *The Outsiders'* continuing popularity over the three plus decades since its publication is the degree to which Hinton captures the emotional turbulence of adolescence. Although readers may not have shared the characters' experiences, many have shared the feelings expressed such as confusion, anxiety, excitement, the general sense of searching, the frustrations of the "in between years."

While many of these feelings are universal, young adolescents are often labeled with a number of stereotypes. They are *troublesome, unpredictable,* and, perhaps, *disrespectful.* Some are *confused, turned off,* or *wild.* While such stereotypes overlook the range of differences among students, they do reflect the view of early adolescence as a time of "storm and stress" that has characterized adolescent psychology for almost 100 years.

Certainly, early adolescence is the time of a great range of major developmental changes. The physical changes are more

1

dramatic in these years than at any other time in the life of a human being, save perhaps for infancy. The sexual changes are a major focal point of their waking hours (and sleeping hours too, in terms of dreams). The social challenges are countless and consume much time and energy. Personal development is erratic, and the likelihood of responsible behavior is totally unpredictable. A school in the middle that is successful is one that is designed around the unique needs of young adolescents. Because these needs are so dynamic and diverse and changing, the middle school culture is extremely complicated. Establishing a sensitive and consistent set of climates in middle level schools is the ultimate challenge to educators.

In fact, a successful school is much like a symphony. As the harmonizing of many parts results in powerful music, so too the appropriate blending of many factors in schools results in powerful experiences for students. Like symphonies, successful schools are different. Each group of students, each staff, each set of dynamics interact to create unique climates for learning. This interaction of factors is especially critical at the middle level. Studies of successful middle schools acknowledge their complexity. The outcomes of their success are like beautiful music. While they capture our attention and draw us close, the underlying "score" is more difficult to describe.

The common theme is clear. **Successful middle schools meet the developmental needs of their students.** The National Middle School Association's position paper *This We Believe: Developmentally Responsive Middle Level Schools* (1995) identifies six foundational characteristics of responsive middle level schools. The first characteristic states

> Effective middle level educators make a conscious choice to work with young adolescents. They understand the developmental uniqueness of young adolescents and are as knowledgeable about their students as they are about the subject matter they teach. Such middle level educators form learning partnerships with their students, demonstrating empathy while engaging them in significant academic learning experiences. (p. 13)

2

This conscious choice to work with and understand their students creates the harmony of the symphony. In the most successful schools, instructional decisions are based on the needs of the student; and the notes, in harmony, produce wonderful music.

However, not all decisions made or all interactions that take place in all middle schools are harmonious. Some decisions, activities, and events reflect discord. They conflict with the needs of students and disrupt the flow of the music. Some of these noises are minor irritants, and they create a distracting "static." Other noises are more disturbing. They promote disharmony, and if accumulated, create such a cacophony that we no longer hear the music. Over time, these episodes can create so much discord that some students become disenchanted and simply tune out.

This new volume continues to explore the "harmony" and "disharmony" of events in the middle grades. Since its predecessor was published over a decade ago, many events and countless innovations in technology have significantly impacted the way schools function. Tragic events involving the use of weapons in schools, along with the rising juvenile crime rate are forcing schools to rethink school safety. Intense pressures from federal, state, and local officials to raise achievement test scores have forced principals and teachers to rethink curriculum, instruction, and assessment practices.

In some cases key middle level concepts such as advisory programs have been abandoned as a direct result of pressure to raise test scores. Technology is progressing at such a rapid rate that teachers often receive on-site staff development from their students who possess both skills and hardware that are more current than what they use in their schools. Television and the media continue to have a tremendous, and largely negative influence on the social and moral development of adolescents. Basketball shoes selling for over $100 are commonly seen on middle school students in both affluent and high poverty schools. *Turning Points 2000: Educating Adolescents in the 21st Century* (Jackson & Davis, 2000) reaffirms the urgency of these developmental issues.

There are more than 19 million young adolescents ages 10-14 in the United States. Approximately 20 percent of them live below the poverty line and nearly 30 percent are members of minority groups (Carnegie Council, 1995). Society, culture, populations, and individuals continually evolve and grow, for better or worse, yet the essence of adolescence remains suspended in time. Somehow, through all this, adolescents continue to be adolescents. Stevenson (1998) provides five key insights that help guide successful practice. These propositions are based on over 30 years of his experience working with youth.

1. Every child wants to believe in himself or herself as a successful person
2. Every youngster wants to be liked and respected
3. Every youngster wants to do and learn things that are worthwhile
4. Every youngster wants physical exercise and freedom to move
5. Youngsters want life to be just (pp. 4-8)

In preparing this publication, we have also incorporated the concept of "developmental assets" advanced by Benson, Galbraith, and Espeland (1998). In their book, *What Kids Need to Succeed*, the authors report the results of a survey of more than 100,000 young people. Responses to this survey convey the reality that young adolescents are healthier, happier, and more successful when they have a larger number of developmental assets. The authors explain this terminology by observing that

> ...the things we identified – building blocks for human development – act like assets in a young person's life. They increase in value over time. They provide a sense of security. They are resources upon which a child can draw again and again. They help young people to make wise decisions, choose positive paths, and grow up competent, caring, and responsible. Also, they are cumulative, meaning that *the more assets a young person has, the better.* (p. 3).

These assets cluster into the following eight categories:

External Assets	Internal Assets
Support	Commitment to Learning
Empowerment	Positive Values
Boundaries and Expectations	Social Competencies
Constructive Use of Time	Positive Identity

These categories will be used to synthesize the research findings in the final chapter. At the same time, the reader will sense the importance of these dynamics in all of the chapters on development.

We examine herein the essence of early adolescence in an era of dramatic change. We first present the highlights of our updated findings about the needs of young adolescents and relate this information to school practices. We describe the "harmony" that is generated when students' needs are addressed and the "discord" that is produced when events conflict with those needs. In the final chapter, we relate our suggestions to a set of eight clusters of essential needs shared by all middle level students. To ensure that what we say is grounded in the realities of the period of early adolescence, we include a series of vignettes that convey what middle level students and teachers think and feel. These vignettes are taken from formal and informal interviews of students and teachers.

When these examples convey harmony, the symbol ⒣ will be used. When the vignette represents disharmony, the symbol ⒟ will be used. Finally, when the illustration simply sheds light on what it is like to live as a young adolescent – reality – this symbol will be used ⒭.

We believe this publication will increase readers' understanding of this critical period of development and serve as an effective means of examining school practices, that readers will have a richer appreciation of the music they hear and, perhaps, a "better ear" for detecting discord and dealing with it before it leads to disruption. ❧

1. Physical Development

Young adolescents are very concerned with their physical and sexual development. For some, physical development or lack thereof is **the** dominant, central theme in their lives. While most middle grades teachers know this to be true, many neglect to make allowances for this "developmental override" when they prepare for their classes. As a result, many students tune in to their personal concerns and tune out even the best teachers. So often, directions have to be repeated, explanations have to be restated, and content has to be retaught because students "flipped out" of the instructional activities while focusing on a physical or sexual concern.

TEACHER: *It's amazing what happens over a long weekend or Christmas vacation. Some of my students come back and it seems that they are two or three inches taller. I have seen students trip over their own feet because their size twelve shoes don't fit their one-hundred and twenty-pound bodies.*

TEACHER: *I've taught at all three grade levels and it never ceases to amaze me how a number of my sixth graders look as young as eight years old and a few of my eighth graders look older than some of the new teachers in the building.*

This kind of developmental override constantly occurs in the classroom. Educators have to be aware of the root causes of these events so that they can make appropriate modifications and allowances in their instruction. Since the basic causes are physical and are directly related to a wide range of social, personal, and intellectual reactions, an overview of the latest research findings in these areas is provided here. Implications for teaching and learning are woven into this overview.

Perhaps the best way to begin this profile is to suggest that the reader try to envision the changes occurring in him/her that commonly occur during early adolescence. For example, how would the typical teacher react to a substantial outbreak of acne including a sizable pimple (or a huge zit in their terms) on the end of the nose? Though it is not possible for adults to completely get into the mind-set of young adolescents, it is important to try because the effort alone may lead to better understanding of their needs. Internalizing and reflecting on common physical changes is one way of walking in the shoes of young adolescents.

Height and weight

The average gain in height is from two to four inches per year, and the average weight gain for young adolescents per year is eight to 10 pounds. Over the early adolescence period, roughly from ages 10 to 15, this averages out to a gain of 10 to 20 inches in height and 40 to 50 pounds (NMSA, 1982,1992; Balk, 1995). And these height and weight increases often come in irregular growth spurts and at varying rates of speed. If the reader gained that much weight over five years, it would typically be viewed as a serious concern. It would lead first to panic and then to dieting, medication, exercise, and could contribute to high blood pressure or heart disease.

INTERVIEWER: *I can see both of you have done some growing lately. Has there been a time you remember noticing how much you'd grown?*

STUDENT A: *I've grown six inches since I started middle school. Just today I saw this girl I always thought was so tall. Today I was almost a head bigger than she was. (Male, age 13, 8th grade)*

STUDENT B: *One month I swear I grew three inches. I knew it because I remembered my height when we were measured at the beginning of the year. Then later we were in the gym and being measured for the scoliosis testing. I saw I measured 5'6". I asked when was the date of the last time I was measured. She said a month ago. I told my Mom because I worried that something might be wrong since it was so fast. Mom said, "Well you're in your big growth spurt. That's normal for a boy your age." That made me feel okay.* (Male, age 14, 9th grade)

Our reaction to such a weight gain by young adolescents may be "No problem, this is happening in the way it should." We also assume that middle grades students understand that their weight gain is natural – but they don't. They worry about these changes and believe that something may be wrong with them, thus having a significant impact on their identity (Woolfolk, 1998).

In a sense, the averages cited are misleading. They convey a good overview but ignore variations within the young adolescent group. In the case of physical development, the differences between young adolescents probably pose more of a problem than the substantial height and weight gains that are typical for 10-15-year-olds. For example, it is possible for a male student to be 5'5" tall and weigh 115 pounds in the sixth grade and have little or no change in height or weight through the seventh, eighth, and even ninth grades. At the same time, another male sixth grader may be 5'9" and weigh 145 pounds and increase in height and weight by the ninth grade to 6'1" and 180 pounds. It is also likely that many girls will be taller than the boy who is 5'5",

Girls, highly conscious of their appearance, are likely to be taller than their boy age-mates.

which further compounds the problems of the smaller male. This has implications for the classroom.

INTERVIEWER: *You had a real problem in Mrs. M's class with Bobby the other day. What was that all about?*

STUDENT: *Bobby's a real wise guy. Last year he was bigger than me and was pushing me around. Well, this year I got bigger than him. I let him know that he couldn't push me around anymore, so he mouths off in class to me, and I get into trouble for talking cause they don't see him. Well, Mrs. M. jumped on me for talking in class, and Bobby started to laugh at me, so I gave him a kick as I went past him to sharpen my pencil. Mrs. M. caught me, and sent me to the office. Next thing I know I spent the rest of the day in I.S.S., and the next day too. But that's all right. Bobby won't mess with me anymore.* (Male, age 14, 8th grade)

Research and our own observations confirm that young adolescents continually compare themselves to others (NMSA, 1982, 1995; Farmer, Farmer, & Gut, 1999). This comparison often leads to a high level of incongruence and dissatisfaction with body image (Kostanski & Gullone, 1998). If they are bigger or smaller, shorter or taller than what they perceive to be the norm, young adolescents tend to think that there is something wrong with them. If they deviate from the norm, then they think that they are abnormal. Middle grades students spend a lot of time worrying about their physical differences – at home and at school during classes.

Disproportionate growth

Growth in young adolescents does not take place evenly. That is, certain parts of the body, most notably the extremities, develop earlier and more rapidly. The young sixth grade male who is 5'9" may wear size 13 shoes which often seem like gunboats to him (and everyone else). His feet are simply too big for the rest of his body. The same is true of hands since hands grow more rapidly too. This obviously affects movement, and it is common to observe a young adolescent tripping over his own feet or reaching across the lunch table for something and spilling milk or catsup or anything in the way. The unhappy reality is that they used to be able to walk or reach out without embarrassing themselves, but now these same simple movements often lead to falls, spills, or other undesirable outcomes. When we add to this the more rapid growth of the nose and ears in comparison to the rest of the body, it is not surprising that our students feel like "Bozo the Clown" and think that their bodies have betrayed them.

Bone growth

Adolescence is also a time when the majority of bone formation occurs (Baker & Cochrane, 1999). During this period bone growth surpasses muscle growth. That is, the skeletal structure is extending more rapidly than the muscular structure. Since muscles support and protect bones, it is more common for young adolescents to experience bone damage such as fractures or breaks. It is also possible to overextend the capacity of the muscular structure causing permanent damage to muscle fibers. As an example, many readers may be aware of a young male who was a "star" pitcher at 12 years old, but because he was pushed beyond reasonable limits, lost most of the power in his arm and could not even pitch on a high school team. Pushing young adolescents to their "limits" may ultimately lead to lower skill performance in the long run and may cause physical harm as well.

Ossification

During early adolescence, the skeletal structure also begins to harden. Recent studies (Amshler, 1999; Pinkowish & Saunders, 1998; Baker & Cochrane, 1999) emphasize the importance of calcium intake for adolescents to increase bone density in order to successfully achieve rapid growth. It is safe to assume that adolescents do not consider the short and long-term effects of reduced calcium intake such as an increased risk of fractures and osteoporosis. What they do understand, however, is that during this rapid bone growth period they are often very uncomfortable. In particular, during this time, the tailbone takes on its final form; three bones fuse together and harden in the posterior area and form the "mature" tailbone. In the process, our students, sitting in hard wooden desks, wiggle their way through classes and this often painful, physical transition. It is also true that the sciatic nerve is closely positioned to the skeletal structure and intensifies student discomfort thus challenging teachers in their attempts to retain the attention of students.

INTERVIEWER: *A number of students made reference to the uncomfortable furniture in the classroom. They would prefer taller desks so that "your knees don't hit the top and make the desk rock." Physical discomfort certainly does not enhance the learning process.*

As this process continues, students also acquire kneecaps. It is true that all children have knees – but not kneecaps. If the reader doubts this, compare your knee to the knee of a son or daughter who is under ten. Yours could be a bit knobby, perhaps too knobby, and a young child's will have a hard surface but no definite cap. Kneecaps are bestowed (for free) on young adolescents. They don't wake up one morning, look down at their legs and exclaim, "Oh, I've got kneecaps." But kneecaps do develop over a period of months during this stage. The cartilage and sinew around the knees coalesce and ossify to form a protective device for this critical joint.

To comprehend the full impact of these processes, the reader might wish to compare the way young adolescents sit and move when given the opportunity to choose where and how to sit as compared to the way they sit in school. If they sit in a chair at home, it is not a hard, wooden one. Actually, many young adolescents lounge on the floor, move around a lot, and create a wide variety of lotus-like positions only using chairs for their feet. It really should not surprise us that middle years students wiggle and fidget a lot in school. They are so uncomfortable that they need to move their bodies around in a never-ending quest to feel comfortable.

Perspiration

LANGUAGE ARTS TEACHER: *You can always tell the hallway where seventh graders are located. A mixture of body odor, cologne,*

and deodorant lingers in the air. The kids come back from P.E.
still sweating from playing basketball. This may sound strange,
but the smell doesn't seem to bother the kids as much as it does
the teachers.

We have "jokingly" told grown-ups that children perspire –
some in great quantities when they're very active. Their perspiration does lead to an unpleasant smell, an odor. At the same time,
parents do not expect their six-year-old son or daughter to wear
deodorant. It's not needed. As children enter early adolescence,
armpit perspiration increases. Sweat and sex glands become very
active and emit odors that are not just unpleasant – they are
offensive. Perspiration may be too polite a term to use; the term
sweat seems to catch the full implication of the locker room odor
that drifts into classrooms with the students. Now, parents
voluntarily buy deodorant for their growing youngsters. Teachers
even resort to using fans to circulate air and blow odors out of
classrooms, especially on hot days.

Hormonal changes

The pituitary glands generate increases in hormones. This
serves as a catalyst for more rapid growth and also as a controller
of glands that determine tissue growth and function. Unfortunately, control of the other glands such as the adrenal glands is
irregular. The irregular control is unfortunate because it leads to
the secretion of adrenaline in "huge" quantities when it is not
needed at all. For example, as a student dutifully works on
twenty square root problems at her seat, she receives an adrenaline secretion that is substantial enough for her to run the length
of a football field ten times without stopping. This hormonal
secretion is akin to an electrical power surge, and it makes the
student squirm and want to move, stretch, and perhaps yell at
the top of her lungs. However, she is expected to work quietly on
square roots. Only the most self-disciplined young adolescent can
sit quietly at times like this.

Nutrition

Some observers affectionately refer to young adolescents'
stomachs as bottomless pits. This is not quite true. The stomach

does become longer, increases in capacity, and the typical middle school student often craves food. This tendency is reinforced by the draining off of nutrients into the rapid growth of body organs. At times, young adolescents are so hungry that "it" hurts. The food has been used up, and they need to replenish their bodies. They will sneak bites off a candy bar fully aware that such is prohibited.

 STUDENT: *I do not want to get fat so I try not to eat everything on the plate but I am so hungry that I always do. See, I want to be a cheerleader and you can't be fat if you are a cheerleader cause they wear short skirts, and everyone could tell that you were too fat because of your skirt. My cousin is a cheerleader, but she is fatter than me so I guess it is okay right now. Next year I am not going to eat all my pizza and maybe get salad and ice cream.* (Female, age 11, 7th grade)

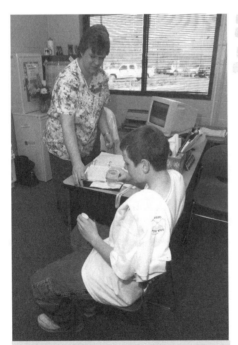

The school clinic is a busy place, especially on Monday mornings.

To compensate for this, students often overload their stomachs by gorging themselves which leads to digestive disturbances. This condition is exacerbated by peculiar eating tendencies of young adolescents. If left unguided, many may eat only fried food, candy, rich desserts, and drink only carbonated beverages. The National Center for Chronic Disease Prevention and Health Promotion (1999) reported that almost three-fourths of young people do not eat the recommended number of servings of fruits and vegetables.

A study conducted by the Federal Interagency Forum on Child and Family Statistics

(1999) concluded that most American children and adolescents had a diet that was poor or needed improvement. The research reports that only six percent of teenagers ages 13 to 18 had a good diet. We believe that fast food lines in schools, specifically fried foods, contribute to this problem. A poor diet can seriously detract from a student's performance in school.

Teachers often observe two patterns in relation to student nutrition. First, a number of students come to school in the morning without ever eating breakfast. These students often appear lethargic from lack of sleep or nutrition and have a limited attention span. They then return from lunch often on a brief "sugar high." For many of these students the last period is a battle to stay awake. The second pattern is evident among those students who eat a well-balanced breakfast and lunch. These students seem to spend more time on task and are usually more active in the instructional phase of the lesson. Teachers often have to adjust and revise class schedules around student nutritional habits. Increasingly schools provide free or minimal cost breakfasts or teachers supply, usually at their own cost, juice and breakfast food, and this has alleviated the problem in some classrooms. In addition, a number of teachers have begun to address eating concerns as parts of thematic curriculum units (L'Esperance, 1997).

When we combine the impact of poor nutritional habits with the irregular secretions of hormones and the overproduction of sweat glands, acne, and other skin defects often result. A pimple on the end of one's nose is rarely a laughing matter. Pimples all over the face of a young adolescent can be personally tragic. Since young adolescents are more self-conscious about their appearance than any other age group, their reaction to pimples is similar to their reaction to the bubonic plague. Though worse things could occur, most middle school students with acne think the worst has already occurred.

STUDENT: *Most of all I worry about my complexion. It is always breaking out. My mom takes me to a dermatologist and sometimes it is better than others, but it is a real problem most of the time. The dermatologist told me I might have this problem until*

I am 21. I don't even want to think about it. I also wanted to wear braces because all my friends were wearing them. I guess that sounds silly to a grown-up. (Male, age 14, 9th grade)

Hair

TEACHER: *When you notice that one of your students comes to school with a new haircut, you've got to be careful. It's like playing "Russian Roulette." If you bring attention to the student and give a compliment in front of his or her peers, you may get a positive response or in some cases group laughter. This can be devastating to anyone, never mind that it is a 13-year-old whose self-concept is so fragile. I've always taken the approach to be safe and issue the compliment in semiprivacy.*

Arth (1992) surveyed a number of middle school students in different settings soliciting their reactions to themselves and their school experiences. When they were asked, "What one thing would you like to change about yourself?" his findings indicated the majority would change their hair. Their hair was too long, too short, too curly, too straight, too full, etc. – but it was consistently unacceptable as it is. This may explain why middle school students continually fiddle with their hair. It just isn't right, and since it is so readily visible, hair has to be worked on to make it look better – whatever better is.

TEACHER: *When I asked Ashley why she was late, she said she missed the bus because her hair was being "really stupid and ugly." I noticed that locker time for Ashley is a very big part of her day. When she opens her locker, I see a very organized display of "necessary" beauty products (such as hair spray and goo; various shades of lip gloss; nail polish and remover; cotton balls , and Q-tips), a large mirror on the inside door, numerous bright stickers of butterflies adorn the locker's interior, with tear-out photos of current heartthrobs.*

Conclusion

As young adolescents make their way through the numerous physical changes that are constantly occurring, they believe that someone is always watching them or that they are always on stage. In 1967, David Elkind first referred to this myth as the "imaginary audience." The result of this egotism is that adolescents often form exaggerated beliefs about their own uniqueness because they do not distinguish their thoughts and feelings from what others think and feel (Balk, 1995). While it may be obvious to adults that young adolescents are not always being observed, it is almost impossible to convince young people of this. Perhaps this is why privacy at home in one's own room or some other place becomes so important. The young adolescent can squirrel away out of sight, turn the music up (way up perhaps) close the door, and eliminate the imaginary audience for a little while. Because it is stressful living on stage day after day, this is a way for a young person to escape from the pressure.

Because young adolescents think they are always being watched, they also engage in another peculiar activity that we call "mirror checking". It seems as though middle level students are drawn to mirrors like metal to magnets and will check themselves out in any mirror available as often as they can. We contend that young adolescents do mirror checks every ten minutes or so to see what else has changed since the last time they looked. Has a new freckle surfaced or is a new pimple patch developing? They need to know how they look at all times in case they run into, sometimes literally, anyone they know, especially a member of the opposite sex.

All of these uneven changes may also lead to a rather negative view of "self." The internal message that must run through the minds of many middle level students at an unconscious level goes something like this: "My body has betrayed me. I'm ugly and clumsy. I've got zits and I can't control myself. I'm bigger (or smaller) than everyone else. No one has problems as big as mine and no one could possibly understand me." This unhappy message is a common tune ending on a sour note. Typical adolescents believe that their stories are so unique and their troubles so great and different that no one, especially adults, can appreciate their needs, interests, or concerns. This myth called "egocentrism" places the middle level student in a world that is lonely and frightening. Educators who keep these physical changes in mind and understand this myth and its impact will be much more effective.

2. Sexual Development

I n the last twenty years television shows, commercials, movies, and pop music have combined to create an image of adolescents as social animals trying to understand sexuality by any means possible. This influence ranges from the innocence of an adolescent's first kiss on a television show to clothing advertisements that depict young males and females in provocative poses accentuating their bodies. Ask typical seventh grade students what the majority of their friends watch on television, and they are quick to respond that MTV and a number of shows with explicit sexual content are their top choices.

The World Wide Web for all its educational potential has also become a cornucopia of sites that provides access to hard-core pornography, adults-only sites, and other influences detrimental to adolescent behavior. An in-depth examination of these shows, programs, and web sites conveys an attitude towards sexuality that embarrasses and angers many parents. Developing ways to address the issues that preoccupy and puzzle young adolescents in regard to sex and their sexuality can make a major difference in the level of harmony or disharmony of a school.

Puberty

As children move into early adolescence, sexual changes begin to occur that are of the utmost interest to them. The major change is that the primary sex hormones, estrogen and testosterone, are produced by two stimulating hormones – the follicle stimulating hormone (FSH) and the luteinizing hormone (LH). When the levels of these two stimulating hormones increase, an individual's gonads (primary sex glands – the ovaries and testes) begin to mature (Balk, 1995). There is tremendous variation in

Discussions about sexual development in groups elicit varied reactions.

the onset of these changes and how rapidly they take place. These differences in sexual development pose a great deal of concern and anxiety. Because of the compelling tendency to compare self to others, young adolescents, especially females, can inevitably develop negative feelings about their bodies (O'Dea & Abraham, 1999). If they use their parents as models of what they should be, they judge themselves to be less endowed (at least, in most cases). If they observe the differences between themselves and older brothers or sisters, they also "lose." Since they typically compare themselves to their peers, they also view themselves as less desirable. If they are smaller in breast development or penis development, they feel less adequate. If they are taller or bigger, they tend to feel self-conscious because they also deviate from the norm. Being bigger usually poses less of a problem than being smaller; however, the main point is, when young adolescents compare themselves to others they inevitably lose. A specific illustration may help.

One of the authors can recall an incident with "Mike the Magnificent" from his own middle years. Mike was a young male, middle level in chronological age, but far far beyond others his age in sexual development. He was very muscular, very hairy, very sizable, and very proud of himself. When we took group showers at school, most of us would skulk around keeping our meager selves covered with towels. Not Mike. Mike would strut around without cover or inhibition very proud of his accouterments. This certainly didn't help the rest of us in coming to terms with our less endowed bodies. To this day, Mike remains emblazoned in my mind as an example of what most of us would never become.

It is assumed that for every Mike, there is a "Barbie," a female counterpart. If this is the case, it is not surprising that young adolescents, very anxious about their sexual development, may feel rather intimidated by these models. It is also not surprising that some students refuse to dress out so they avoid being embarrassed by their "allegedly" underdeveloped bodies. Because our society has placed such a heavy emphasis on this area and reinforces perfection in sexual appearance through the media, young people suffer for no good reason. They judge themselves to be inadequate because they compare themselves with role models that don't represent how most people look.

INTERVIEWER: *What do you like least about your school?*

STUDENT A: *I don't like P.E. I guess I especially don't like the showers. None of the kids shower here. I haven't seen one kid take a shower since I've been here. They have nice showers in the gym, but no one uses them. Luckily I have P.E. seventh period and if I'm all hot and sweaty, I can shower when I get home.* (Male, age 13, 9th grade)

STUDENT B: *I don't like the showers in P.E. No one uses the showers. The teachers don't make us shower. They know we don't like it. Some of the guys shower in their underwear. Can you imagine sitting around all day in wet clothes? It's awful. I tried this, but now I don't shower at school.* (Male, age 14, 9th grade)

The reality is that a wide range of sexual development exists, and variations should be accepted as normal. We should provide factual data to communicate this fact to our students. It may be one of the more helpful contributions we could make to young adolescents. The following overview of the variations in sexual development and related commentary will provide information that can be shared with students.

The events of puberty in girls and boys

About half of all girls have begun breast development at age $11^{1/2}$. Half will have pubic hair at age $11^{1/2}$. About 50 percent have begun to menstruate by age $12^{3/4}$. Menstruation usually occurs approximately one year after breast, uterine, and vaginal development. The average age for growth of the penis is $12^{1/4}$ years and it is $12^{1/2}$ years for the appearance of pubic hair. These changes occur approximately one year following the growth of the testes and scrotum (Balk, 1995). It is important to note that these ages are central tendencies in a wide age range. Half have become involved in the event by the average age *and* half have not. A look at the ranges of the various events may be more informative.

According to data reported by Farel (1982), some girls begin breast development as early as $8^{3/4}$ years and as late as $13^{1/4}$ years of age. Pubic hair may appear as early as nine years and as late as $13^{1/2}$ years. Some girls may begin to menstruate at the age of $10^{3/4}$, and others may not experience menstruation until $15^{1/2}$ years of age. For boys, testes enlargement may occur as early as $9^{1/2}$ and as late as $13^{1/2}$, and growth of the penis may begin as early as age 10 and as late as the age of 14. The appearance of pubic hair may occur as early as $9^{1/2}$ years and as late as age 14. McLean's (1998) research on sexual development reveals that by age ten, 68 percent of white American girls and 95 percent of African American girls show signs of puberty (breast development or pubic hair development). These ranges are extensive and are important to recognize. Young adolescent girls and boys need to know some basic facts about sexual development and the ranges of the events of puberty. Hockenberry-Eaton and Richman's (1996) study on adolescent knowledge of sexual development revealed that adolescents were unable to adequately define most of the basic sexual development terms. This lack of knowledge makes educators, not television shows and music videos, the individuals in the best position to provide factual information.

INTERVIEWER: *When sex education is going to be taught, are boys and girls separated?*

STUDENT: *Well, we were separated in the 6th grade, but not in the 7th grade. Everyone was together for the same stuff.*

INTERVIEWER: *Did anyone get embarrassed? Did you feel uncomfortable about asking questions?*

STUDENT: *Yeah, most of the kids did get really embarrassed about all of the stuff with guys and the girls in the same class. We really didn't want to ask a lot of questions.* (Male, age unknown, 8th grade)

One assurance that middle grades boys and girls need to have is that everything will take place in its own time. Nature keeps its own biological clock, and the timing, whether one likes it or not, can't be changed. Sexual development will occur in its own good time. No one needs to feel bad if his/her development does not occur at the rate or time that he/she wants it to occur; it is beyond a person's control. In the same way, young adolescents who are bigger or smaller in terms of sexual features are not better – they have just developed that way. This last statement needs to be said as convincingly and as often as possible, but it still probably won't be believed.

 STUDENT: *I hate P.E. because it is really boring. We just learn the rules to the games but never get much time to play. We have to dress out in P.E. and that is kind of embarrassing. Our teacher is mean and she calls you by your last name.* (Female, age 12, 8th grade)

It is also important to help these young people understand a few other facts about some of these events. For example, girls may begin to menstruate, but their periods may be very irregular. It is interesting to note that many young females are most eager to "start" but this eagerness seems to rapidly dissipate after the first period. It may be two years before a regular adult cycle is established. Boys may be interested in knowing that the enlargement of the testes is almost always the first event of puberty for them, not the appearance of pubic hair as is commonly thought.

STUDENT: *I think there should be more sex education. We study sex, but I think it should be stressed more. Sometimes when we're studying it, people will laugh. I think it should be offered through science. Health is considered more of a fun thing because it's mixed in with gym. If it were offered in science maybe people wouldn't laugh so much because they'd be getting a more serious grade.*

INTERVIEWER: *That's a good idea. Are the boys and girls in the same class?*

STUDENT: *Sometimes. We didn't discuss sex together, but we saw some of the films together about when a girl grows up and when a boy grows up. We studied the adolescent changes together.*

INTERVIEWER: *What did they tell you about adolescent changes?*

STUDENT: *It was okay, but boys are so silly. They had to laugh at everything. They want to see the girl's film with the girls, but they didn't want to see the boy's film with the girls.*

INTERVIEWER: *Do you think they were embarrassed?*

STUDENT: *They were being silly!* (Female, age 12, 8th grade)

Sexual activity and pregnancy

This is an issue that must be discussed as a part of adolescent sexual development. A number of research studies verify the trend over the last several decades toward increased sexual activity at a younger age. It is estimated that 80 percent of male youths and 70 percent of young females in this country have had sexual intercourse prior to leaving the teen years. Of this group, the only age group in which the pregnancy rate is still markedly increasing is the under 15 age group. Balk's (1995) review of research indicates that adolescents have increasingly become involved in more casual, less committed sexual activity. With the reality of HIV and other sexually transmitted diseases, this is a serious problem that must be addressed. Helping young males and females to be more sexually aware and responsible is a necessity.

Sexual preference

It is clear that many young adolescents struggle with their sex role identity. They are also uncertain about what is normal. For example, same sex friendship is the dominant pattern for this age group, but it generates concern for some young people. They may think that their preference for being friends with members of the same sex is abnormal. In reality, it is perfectly appropriate, but society places such an emphasis on getting along with the opposite sex that they feel uneasy about doing what is natural.

Young adolescents also worry because their bodies behave in a peculiar manner at times. For some boys, an erection may occur at a most undesirable time (e.g. in math or language arts class) for no apparent reason. Girls may be sexually stimulated and also embarrassed in a similar manner at a similar time. Young males and females need to know that these episodes may occur to some and not to others, but that they needn't be overly concerned. Above all, they need to understand that they are not "gay" simply because such an event occurs.

Sexually transmitted diseases

One final area needs to be discussed briefly. Reliable data available on the World Wide Web on adolescence and sexually transmitted diseases reinforce the need for middle schools to conduct discussions related to sexual development with their students. Sobering statistics indicate that in the U.S., more than 12 million new cases of sexually transmitted diseases (STDs) occur each year, with at least three million of them among teenagers. As of 1997, 612,0078 cases of AIDS have been reported to the Centers for Disease Control (CDC), and of these people, 379,258 had died by the end of June 1997 (*Journal of American Medical Association*, 2000, http:/jama.ama-assn,org/).

The Centers for Disease Control (2000) also reports

1. The United States has the highest teen pregnancy rate among developed countries
2. One million teenagers become pregnant each year; 95 percent are unintended; 33 percent end in abortion
3. Birth rates during 1991-96 declined for teenagers in all racial and ethnic groups
4. Compared with 1991, sexual experiences are more prevalent
5. Each year, approximately three million cases of sexually transmitted diseases (STDs) occur among teenagers

— http://www.cdc.gov./

Conclusion

Television, cinema, and music, have all conveyed a series of "misconceptions" to young adolescents about their own sexuality. A great deal of confusion exists in their minds about the events of puberty. Yet these events play a dominant role in the way young adolescents think, feel, and behave, and they deserve to be properly informed. Educators need to debunk myths and provide a solid base of factual information. Teachers also need to be available to listen to students and provide guidance in sexual development so students will know what to say and do in relating to members of the opposite sex. This kind of assistance can provide an invaluable service to young adolescents as they struggle to understand their own sexuality.●

3. Intellectual Development

While not as observable as physical changes, the intellectual changes that occur during early adolescence are equally dramatic. It is during this period that students first develop powers of abstract reasoning. They begin to think of the world around them in new ways. They also begin to think of themselves in new ways. For the first time in their lives, most young adolescents can "think about thinking" – and that often confuses them. These new powers of reasoning allow them to form sophisticated self-concepts that are shaped by interactions between their experiences and their thoughts about them. Classroom activities play a major role in this process. When teachers understand how reasoning develops and can interpret students' responses accordingly, they are able to orchestrate activities in ways that promote harmony.

The development of abstract reasoning

One of the most powerful theories explaining the nature of intellectual changes is Piaget's stage theory of mental development. Piaget (1972) suggests that mental development occurs in four distinct phases. Each child passes through the stages in the same sequence, but at varying rates. The logical operations of each stage develop from the operations of the previous stage. Within this framework, early adolescence is a period of transition from the "concrete operations" stage to the "formal operations" stage, a stage that may begin for some as early as the eleventh year. Figure 1 (p. 28) presents an overview of the transition from concrete to formal operations.

FIGURE 1

Young Adolescent Reasoning: A Time of Transition

AGE 7 - 11	10 - 14	13 - ??
Development of concrete reasoning	Time of transition	Development of formal operations
"Logical thinking about things"	"Mastery of concrete operations, Experimentation with formal operations."	"Thinking with abstractions"

CLUES

Classification	Creating Theories	Hypothetical-
Conservation	Thinking about	deductive
"Arithmetic"	thinking	reasoning

DIFFICULTIES

Abstract ideas	Empathy	Applications
Complex verbal problems	Patience	and transfer
Suspending judgments	Synthesis	

Students in the concrete operations stage develop the ability to carry out logical operations on concrete objects. They can reverse processes, distinguish between concepts, and relate ideas in a serial fashion. They can thus solve mathematical or logical problems presented in concrete situations where they can manipulate material data they can see and touch. Logical operations in the abstract are not yet possible.

As students enter the period of formal operations, they begin to be able to reason logically about verbal statements in the absence of particular objects. "This period is characterized in general by the conquest of a new mode of reasoning, one that is no longer limited exclusively to dealing with objects or directly representable realities, but also employs 'hypotheses'" (Piaget, 1970, p. 33). During formal operations, students can begin to deal with such mathematical concepts as permutations, combinations, probabilities, and correlations. They can also begin to use language as a medium for expanding thinking. In other words, they can now join reading and thinking together in propositional thinking. They become quite capable of reflecting on life experiences in and out of school.

STUDENT: *During my spare time I just eat and watch TV. When I get bored, I just sit around and wait for my dad or bug my brother, I like shows about police and crime as well as MTV. I do my homework on the bus in the morning or if my dad remembers to ask, I'll just do a little for him to check. He's busy. I usually don't remind him to sign my planner. It's so stupid. Why do we need those things? I ain't no child. I don't like getting checked every day.* (Male, age 12, 7th grade)

INTERVIEWER: *An eighth grade student, Kasey, talked to the teacher about bringing in her homework tomorrow. After the teacher said "fine," Kasey whispered to her friend, "I knew I could get away with it." Her friend laughed. Ten minutes into the lesson, Kathy raised her hand and asked to go the bathroom, claiming an emergency. When she came back, she took a long time to find her place and resume her conversation with her friend.* (Female, age 13, 8th grade)

The development of formal operations is not a continuous process of development, however. Only when a student has assimilated and accommodated the actions and operations of one stage can he or she pass on to the next. Moreover, there is wide variation in the ages at which students begin to enter formal operations. Differences in social environment and acquired experiences create wide variations in rates of development. While the average age for beginning formal operations is eleven, Piaget (1972) reports experimental studies showing as much as four years of "time lag" (p. 36). The age range of early adolescence suggests then that within a given grade level, or even a given class, there will be wide variation in the developmental stages of individual pupils – a condition that challenges teachers.

Figure 2 illustrates that variation. Responses from students to a verbal problem of this type demonstrate a range of responses

FIGURE 2
Responses of Fifth and Sixth Grade Students
to a Reading and Thinking Problem

PROBLEM: At a meeting of the television news staff, the weather reporter was told that her material was too dull. That night she made up for it.

Good evening. Today's weather, as you have probably noticed, is different from yesterday's. If the weather is the same tomorrow as it was yesterday, the day after tomorrow will have the same weather as the day before yesterday. But if the weather tomorrow is the same as today, the day after tomorrow will have the same weather as yesterday. As you know, it's raining today, and it rained on the day before yesterday.

QUESTION: Was it raining or clear yesterday?

(*Thinklab.* Science Research Associates, 1974)

STUDENT RESPONSES:

Tom:	It's raining because the story implied it.
David:	Clear – it said so in the story.
Evan:	Clear – because it was clear every other day.
Wendy:	You can't tell because she didn't say what tomorrow will be like.
Shannon:	It was raining yesterday because the weather is the same as tomorrow and tomorrow is the same as today and it's raining today.
Rob:	It will be clear because she said that today is raining and if she had said that tomorrow would be raining she could have said tomorrow would be the same as yesterday.

Christie:

Day before Yesterday	Yesterday	Today	Tomorrow	Day after Tomorrow
*	?		?	*
Raining		Raining		

So yesterday was clear.

Daryl:	Clear yesterday because of rain today.
Marc:	If today's weather is different from yesterday's and it is raining today, it was clear yesterday.

from Tom's random guess to Marc's very sophisticated propositional statement. Responses also demonstrate stage differences as well. Christie used a concrete sequential strategy to solve the problem while Marc analyzed the problem in a very formal way.

Studies of the development of formal reasoning suggest that approximately one-third of eighth graders consistently demonstrate formal abilities (Strahan, 1986). These studies have far-reaching implications for curriculum and instruction. Middle level teachers should carefully consider the reasoning levels of students when planning instruction and designing lessons that match student readiness levels (Strahan & Toepfer, 1984; Milgram, 1992). More importantly, the distribution of reasoning development for a given class or grade level is very difficult to predict. Not only is there variability among students in the acquisition of formal reasoning (Woolfolk, 1998) but there is some evidence that there is variability within individuals as well. Smart and Smart (1973) and Balk (1995) suggest that the development of formal operations is uneven across subject matter areas and is often situational. The adolescent may be able to think abstractly in one area but not in another. Adolescents often experience varying attention spans, demonstrating both a sense of urgency and a tendency to act as if time were not important. These variations in internal development further suggest a sense of "unevenness" in thinking helping us understand the wide range of individual differences likely to occur in any given classroom at any given time.

TEACHER OBSERVER: *As math class begins, Carly immediately took out her homework and started reviewing it with the two boys sitting at her table. She told them that one of their answers was wrong and made a bet with them that she was right. When the teacher reviewed the homework, she raised her hand for every question. When the teacher assigned a new worksheet, her behavior changed dramatically. She began to stress out over completing the assignment on time. The other students completed it and turned it in without many hassles. She was the last to turn it in and kept going over it until the bell rang. When I asked her about it after class, she seemed angry. "She*

When we consider the level of abstraction required by many of the concepts commonly found in a middle school curriculum, instructional planning becomes even more complex. Figure 3 (p. 33) provides a sample of such concepts.

Approaching these concepts in a meaningful way often requires teachers to help students make connections between the concrete ideas they already understand and these new abstractions. Teaching these formal concepts without careful planning can make learning even more difficult for students. The integration of learning from one subject area to another facilitates mastery of new abstract concepts for students. Curriculum integration is clearly in line with the intellectual development of young adolescents and will assist students in achieving the stage of formal operations.

STUDENT: *I liked science and math. I usually got A's in these subjects. This last year I took algebra. I didn't understand it. The teacher didn't explain it right. She'd go through a whole problem, give us homework, and then the next day she'd give us a test. I just didn't get it. I'm taking algebra next year again when I'm in the ninth grade.* (Male, age 13, 8th grade)

Understanding how formal reasoning develops over time helps teachers plan instruction that encourages students to try new modes of reasoning without penalizing those still unable to make abstract connections.

TEACHER: *What do you like least about school?*

STUDENT: *They've got a lot of rules that don't seem to make a lot of sense to me. Like, why can't we chew gum in school? In some classes, they even give us candy for doing things right, and the school gives candy for a lot of things, but we can't chew gum. That's dumb. And, even though I think it looks dumb, I don't understand why they have such a problem with saggy pants.* (Male, age 13, 8th grade)

FIGURE 3

A sample of abstract concepts taught in the middle grades

LANGUAGE ARTS
Main idea
Metaphor
Parts of speech
Symbolism
Theme

SCIENCE
Conservation of energy
Molecular structure
Photosynthesis
Relativity
Respiration

MATHEMATICS
Algebraic expression
Equations
Ratio
Sets
"Thought problems"

SOCIAL STUDIES
Democracy
Distance (thousands of miles)
Justice
Space (countries, continents)
Time (centuries, millennia)

A more comprehensive view of reasoning development

While Piaget's studies of reasoning development have helped us understand many of the changes that occur during early adolescence, more recent studies of intellectual development offer a broader view of learning and teaching. Hoge's (1999) strong summary of the limitations of Piaget's theory follows.

- Representation of development in terms of passage through qualitatively distinct stages has been questioned by some who suggest that development is simply not that orderly.
- Individuals may show considerable variability across tasks in level of cognitive functioning.
- Piaget's representation of the nature of thought during adolescence is too simplistic.
- Relatively few efforts have been made to translate the descriptive framework into practical assessment instruments.

Fortunately, at the same time that some researchers have examined the accuracy and validity of Piaget's theory, other researchers have explored related realms of reasoning development. As a result, we are learning a great deal about how the brain works and about how young adolescents expand their thinking abilities.

Multiple intelligences

One of the most exciting discoveries has been Gardner's (1983) theory of Multiple Intelligences. His analyses of brain functions and creative processes have documented at least eight ways of understanding. In addition to the more familiar "intelligences" such as linguistic learning, logical reasoning, and spatial development, Gardner has shown that we also use bodily-kinesthetic, musical, naturalistic, and personal intelligences. Teachers of all grades have found that Gardner's framework fits their observations of classroom learning over the years (Strahan, 1985; Strahan & Strahan, 1988). Consequently, Multiple Intelligences is now providing a framework for planning lessons that taps individual talents and involves students in learning about learning. Studies of efforts to put Gardner's theory into practice (Gardner & Hatch, 1989) have documented a number of applications for elementary, middle, and high schools that have proven successful. In reviewing this research, Gardner (1995) identified the essential aspects of good teaching with multiple intelligences.

- Cultivating desired capabilities
- Approaching concepts, subjects, and disciplines in a variety of ways
- Personalizing education (pp. 207-208)

Early adolescence is a critical time in the development of multiple intelligences. As their powers of reasoning grow more sophisticated, young adolescents become more aware of their own unique talents and interests. Some students find that they have a real talent for music, or art, or movement, or nature. Others learn that they learn best when they work with groups or by themselves. Many find that they learn best through a combination of intelligences. When parents and teachers support their efforts to try out new ideas and new modes of reasoning, students begin to take more ownership of the learning process. A key element in this progression is the gradually increasing ability to think about thinking.

Thinking about thinking

INTERVIEWER: *What would you like to change?*

 STUDENT: *The way I act when someone asks me to do something; because most of the time I will talk back and get into trouble, and I don't want to get into trouble.*

(Male, age 14, 8th grade)

As adults, we often take our ability to think about our thoughts for granted. We have examined our inner worlds for so long that introspection has become a natural part of who we are. We forget that we were not nearly so aware of our thoughts as children. For example, when we observe preschoolers trying to learn new and challenging tasks, such as tying their shoes, we notice that they may experience bouts of frustration but do not dwell on them. They move on to other tasks and return to shoe tying when prompted to do so. From observations of many episodes like this, we conclude that young children demonstrate a limited awareness of "not understanding."

This awareness grows stronger through the elementary years, and by the time they reach the middle grades, students are keenly aware of times when they do not understand things that others seem to know. In fact, when presented with mental tasks that are too difficult, they may dwell on their inability to perform them. This is especially the case when they see classmates solving problems that they cannot.

One way this becomes an issue in the classroom is reflected in "I could do it if I wanted to" defense mechanism. When faced with tasks that appear to be too difficult, many young adolescents say to themselves, "I could figure this out if I really wanted to but I don't want to." Such a rationalization is much easier than admitting that the task is difficult and may be beyond their present level of reasoning, but this avoidance response prevents some students from taking academic chances. Consequently, they miss opportunities to expand their powers of reasoning, making it more likely that they will be frustrated the next time they face a similar problem. Teachers who are sensitive to this issue can help students approach challenging tasks with less fear of failure.

Resource persons from community agencies elicit responses and enrich the curriculum.

STUDENT: *Math is my favorite because our teacher makes it really fun and I learn a lot. When I was little I wasn't good in math because it was real hard and I never could get my homework right. Now I am good in math, I usually make an A or B in it because I understand it. Our teacher is great because she explains things and doesn't mind if you ask questions even if she has already explained it once. My math teacher's favorite subject is math. You can tell she likes it a lot because she always seems happy when we come to class. We always have homework in math and I don't mind doing it because I can get it right without asking my mom.* (Female, age 12, 8th grade)

One of the most helpful frameworks for understanding how young adolescents think about their thoughts is Glasser's (1986)

Control Theory. Control theory describes ways that students choose their behaviors to fit their pictures of themselves and to meet basic needs for security, belonging, freedom, power, and fun. "Not trying" when a task seems too difficult is a way of preserving psychological security. "Not trying" in order to fit in with others who are not trying may also be an attempt to belong. Sometimes, students assert themselves to bolster a sense of freedom or power. At other times, diversion seems like more fun than participation.

Glasser's studies show that students can form more productive pictures of themselves when they experience success and identify with significant others. Teachers can help students think about their thoughts more productively by encouraging them to consider choices and consequences. Taking time to identify options for decisions and predict the outcomes of these options helps students develop a stronger sense of personal responsibility.

Connecting feelings and thinking

As researchers have discovered new insights about ways of thinking and the powers of introspection, a number of studies have underscored the importance of emotions in the learning process. One of the most helpful summaries of the impact of emotions on learning is Goleman's (1995) *Emotional Intelligence.* His studies of the connections among thoughts and feelings show just how complicated and individualistic reasoning really is. "In reality, the brain's wetware is awash in a messy, pulsating puddle of neurochemicals, nothing like the sanitized, orderly silicon that has spawned the guiding metaphor for mind" (p. 40-41).

Goleman's (1995) descriptions of the ways feelings and thoughts are connected suggest that we need to help students identify feelings, manage feelings appropriately, motivate themselves, and respond to the feelings of others.

Flow theory (Csikszentmihalyi, 1990) provides a powerful framework for understanding how individuals put these thinking dynamics into motion. Csikszentmihalyi (1989) and his colleagues have found that adolescents' involvement in meaningful learning activities is characterized by "flow."

Flow is what people feel when they enjoy what they
are doing, when they would not want to do anything
else. What makes flow so intrinsically motivating?
The evidence suggests a simple answer: in flow, the
human organism is functioning at its fullest capacity.
When this happens, the experience is its own reward.

(p. 55)

In a series of studies conducted with people of all ages from
several different parts of the world, Csikszentmihalyi and his
research team have observed that almost everyone shares some
notion of the concept of "flow." While the nature of the tasks
may vary by age range or interest, all of the people profiled have
reported times when they were so involved in a task that they lost
track of time. This feeling of immersion, whether in reading a
book, climbing a mountain, playing a musical instrument, or
watching a movie, is the essential definition of flow. Participants
in these studies have shared stories of being so engaged with the
moment at hand that they forget to take a break to eat or failed to
remember something important they were supposed to do. These
moments of immersion characterize flow as one of the most
powerful states of mind.

In a particularly intensive study, Csikszentmihalyi and his
colleagues kept track of the daily life of adolescents over a twelve
year period. They asked participants to record their thoughts and
feelings when prompted by beepers that were programmed to go
off at random intervals. During each week of the study, researchers gathered from 30 to 50 "snapshots of daily life" that they used
as a basis for extended interviews with their participants. The
resulting analysis delineated over 100 different activities that
adolescents viewed as enjoyable.

The resulting "flow model" of intrinsic motivation describes key
factors that interact to produce (or inhibit) cognitive engagement.
Csikszentmihalyi (1990) summarizes some of the ways that fifth
and sixth graders reported "flow experiences."

One after the other, these children described what
they enjoyed most about playing the piano, or
swimming, or acting in school plays. One said that

while doing these things, "I can forget my problems." Another said, "I can keep the things that bother me out of my mind" and so on. In class, they claimed, they could seldom achieve such concentration.

(p. 130)

In the classroom, students reported a "vicious circle" of experiences in which they sometimes were not concentrating on the tasks at hand, began to think of other things, and then found it even more difficult to concentrate. Consequently, "even in very good schools students actually pay attention to what is supposed to go on quite rarely" (p. 134). Csikszentmihalyi concludes that flow experiences in academic settings require a sense of "immersion" in the tasks themselves (p. 137). Teachers who "intuitively know that the best way to achieve their goals is to enlist students' interest on their side" and who "do this by being sensitive to students' goals and interests" have the best chance of encouraging such immersion (p. 137).

They empower students to take control of their learning; they provide clear feedback to the students' efforts without making them self-conscious. They help students concentrate and get immersed in the symbolic world of the subject matter. (p. 137).

Csikszentmihaly (1990) insists that teachers play an essential role in encouraging enjoyment.

Basically, young people are influenced by adults who appear to enjoy what they do, and who promise to make the youth's life more enjoyable too. This is not such a bad yardstick to use – why should youth choose models who seem miserable and who strive to impoverish their future? (p. 133)

By understanding more about the nature of students' thoughts when they are naturally engaged in a flow state of mind, teachers can foster conditions that encourage learning that is "mindful."

Mindful learning

Mindful Learning: Teaching Self-discipline and Academic Achievement (Strahan, 1997) is an attempt to synthesize all of these logical, intellectual, and emotional perspectives on reasoning development. Based on work in classrooms with a number of "expert" teachers, mindful learning integrates these theoretical perspectives with the wisdom of practice that has evolved in successful classrooms over time. Figure 4 shows how mindful learning integrates theory and practice.

Figure 4
Theory and Practice of Mindful Learning

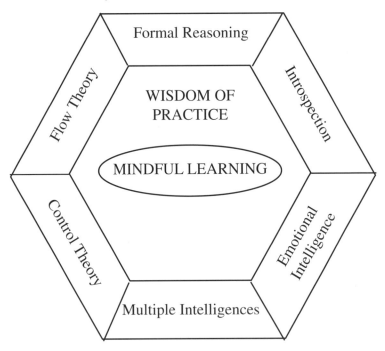

Mindful learning provides a framework for promoting reasoning development that reflects how the mind works best.

Our best information suggests that the mind works from the inside out, extending self-awareness and feelings into the comprehension of other people and external realities. To teach mindfully, we need to appreciate this complexity and recognize the power of emotions. Students are most likely to learn new academic concepts when we address the "feeling tones" of information. They cannot learn self-discipline unless we do so. More than anything else, mindful learning is integrative. By helping students make sense out of their life experiences, mindful learning connects self-awareness with academic understanding. (Strahan, 1997, p. 35)

OBSERVER: *Jennifer is a bright, loud, beautiful 8th grade girl. She is the focal point of attention. She wrote a very poignant poem during a language arts exercise. It centered around the recent divorce of her parents and the emptiness of going home to a house half-full with siblings. It was a real "gut-wrencher" to see how this pain forces a child to reckon with "living grief." Many of the children knew about Jennifer's family problems and defended her in a conflict with a teacher. It was wise of the teacher to back down from the conflict and to give Jennifer space. Other teachers are having trouble with Jennifer. The quickest way to diffuse a situation is to not argue, banter, or push. A better time when the child is rational will come.*

As a synthesis of research on reasoning development, *Mindful Learning: Teaching Self-Discipline and Academic Achievement* (Strahan, 1997) suggests four essential principles for supporting young adolescents' intellectual growth.

- Intellectual development occurs when students make connections between their own needs/interests/feelings and new ideas (personalization)
- Students learn to assume more responsibility for their own learning when they can discuss how they learn best with their classmates (conversation) and when they have opportunities to examine their choices and the consequences of those choices (reflection)
- Students learn best when they have opportunities for "hands on/minds on" problem-solving activities that use

multiple intelligences (variety) and relate to real-world situations (authenticity)

- Students learn best when teachers help them learn specific mental procedures they can rely on when asked to solve new problems. These structures provide a sense of security when students face challenging tasks and provide a framework for connecting new information to prior knowledge (guidance)

Middle school teachers need to challenge – even cajole – their students into stretching their emerging mental abilities.

These principles provide a framework for analyzing classroom practices. Figure 5 presents a summary scale for assessing students' perceptions of their classroom as a place that promotes or inhibits reasoning development.

Conclusions

These descriptions of reasoning development characterize early adolescence as a period of rapid and dramatic changes in thinking, changes that interact with physical development and provide a backdrop for personal and social development as well. Not only do the bodies of young adolescents change, but also new powers of reasoning allow them to reflect upon those changes, dwell upon them, and sometimes even become fixated on them. These

Figure 5
Perceptions of the classroom climate for reasoning

Dimensions of Reasoning Development	Classroom Climates that Promote Reasoning Development	Classroom Climates that Inhibit Reasoning Development
Personalization	"We understand how this topic relates to our lives."	"We see no relationship between this topic and our lives."
Conversation	"We have opportunities to discuss how we learn as much as what we learn."	"All of our discussions are about the subject matter itself."
Reflection	"We are encouraged to think about our choices for making decisions and the consequences of our choices."	"The teacher tells us what we do that is correct and incorrect, right or wrong."
Variety	"For most assignments, we have opportunities to use several types of intelligence to explore issues or complete projects."	"We must all follow one set of directions, exactly the same way."
Authenticity	"We can see connections between activities that we do in class and things that happen in the real world."	"We rarely see any connection between school stuff and what happens in our lives."
Guidance	"If we are not sure how to solve a problem, our teacher shows us specific problems we can try."	"If we are not sure how to solve a problem, we have to rely on trial and error."

new powers of reasoning also mean that young adolescents think in new ways about their relations with other people and their concepts of themselves. Experiences in school are a critical dimension of this development. Academic learning changes as students stretch their new powers of reasoning to understand abstract ideas. Teachers can present challenging ideas in ways that build on students' levels of understanding and encourage them to learn more about their ways of learning. As they do so, they can also enhance identity development, their sense of who they are and how they relate to their world. These themes are the focus of Chapter Four. ◐

4. Social and Personal Development

T he social and personal dimensions of development are inextricably interwoven. Young adolescents don't define themselves in a vacuum. Rather, they define their identity based, to a large extent, on how "significant" others convey their perceptions of them. Parents/caretakers, friends, teachers, and other family members play key roles in their personal development. For this reason, we are including these two areas of development in the same chapter.

 Anthony is not your typical eighth grade student. He will turn 16 years old in a few months. When he is among a group of classmates he may be mistaken for the teacher or another adult in the school. The snake tattoos on both arms accentuate the muscular forearms that have been developed by doing manual labor with his father for several years. His thin mustache reinforces his "man among boys" attitude. As we begin to speak before school one morning, I'm aware that last night's social studies homework is far from the top of his priority list. He already has a two-year-old daughter and thinks his girlfriend may be pregnant again. His parents are threatening to kick him out of the house if he doesn't straighten up his act. However, this morning in the commons area, while several hundred students wait for school to start, I begin to probe Anthony's perceptions of his peers. Listening to our conversation, Anthony sounds more like a graduate student conducting research than an at-risk student whose days in school are numbered.

MR. L.: *Anthony, tell me about some of the different groups of kids who are hanging out in the commons area.*

ANTHONY: *No problem. (He begins to move through the crowd of students who part his path as quickly as they see him approaching) Over there you got the "Home Boys". They think they are bad and some of them do drugs or just say they do drugs. They try to pretend they're gang members and they always get in trouble in school. That group next to them is the "Wannabe Home Boys" who try to hang out with the "homeys" but aren't allowed to. Sometimes some of the "homeys" make the "wannabes" do stupid stuff just so they can watch them get in trouble.*

MR. L.: *How do you become a "Home Boy"?*

ANTHONY: *You got to live in their neighborhood. (He waves to several of the homeys as we walk by. A couple of them look at Tony trying to figure why he is walking around with a teacher. No one questions him openly.) Over there you got the "Preppies." They are the rich kids who live in big houses and always are talking about spending money and going on trips. They're* *nothing but snobs. Most of those girls won't even talk to me. Look at the clothes they wear. I would never buy my clothes from those stupid stores. (The girls in the group pay no attention to Tony as he walks by. The boys in the group deliberately try to avoid Tony's intimidating glare.)*

MR. L: *Anthony, how come this group of "preppies" isn't with the other group?*

ANTHONY: *They ain't "preppies." They're "wannabe preppies". You can always tell a wannabe preppie because they don't wear the same label clothing as the preppies. They can't afford it. Some of them come from the same trailer park as me. (Anthony refuses to recognize a couple of attempts by students in the group to say hello.)*

ANTHONY: *One thing we got at this school Mr. L. is "nerds." We got all kinds of "nerds." Look over there. Those are the "smart*

46

nerds." They get A's on everything they do. They aren't in my
class. They get put in the classes for smart kids. Then you got
your weird nerds. They just stick by themselves and act all
stupid.

Anthony finishes his tour by providing detailed descriptions of the remaining peer group in the school (burnouts, jocks, and loners).

The concept of adolescent identity is far more complex than Anthony's biased descriptions of peer groups. Yet, this eighth grade student, through this ability to analyze identity labels (i.e. peer groups) has an implicit understanding of how stressful and traumatic choosing group relationships can be for identity formation. In response to the turbulent changes they experience in their physical and intellectual development, young adolescents experience dramatic changes in self-concept. More than anything else, young adolescents need to develop views of themselves as valuable, able, and responsible people (Purkey & Strahan, 1986).

Psychologists have long viewed the formation of self-concept during early adolescence as a search for identity. Suggesting, "identity is the central theme of adolescence," Josselson (1994) defines identity as the adolescent's search for claiming membership in the social world, standing for something, being known for who one is. This search consists of both process and product. Identity acts as "an unfolding bridge" linking individual and society, childhood, and adulthood. Building on Erikson's (1968) theory of identity development, Roesser, Eccles, and Sameroff (2000) suggest an integrative perspective on "psychosocial identity" that links the development of young adolescents' views of who they are with the levels of support offered them by their families, schools, and communities.

> His (Erikson's) 1968 treatise on adolescent identity
> was meant to draw attention to his contention that an
> adolescent's ability to organize the significant
> changes they experience during these years into a
> coherent and positive psychosocial identity was not
> simply a personal project but rather a collective and

47

intergenerational responsibility of the adolescent and his or her parents, teachers, and community members. (p. 444)

Analysis of data from a longitudinal study of almost 1500 young adolescents and their families in the Maryland Adolescent Development in Context Study shows that three essential aspects of adolescents' lives in school contexts shape their views of themselves, their social-emotional functioning and their success in school: 1) how well their experiences support a sense of competence; 2) how well their experiences support a sense of autonomy; and 3) the quality of their relationships with peers and adults (Roesser, Eccles, & Sameroff, 2000).

Opportunities to interact with peers under the direction of a teacher meet a clear social need.

A sense of competence

In almost every respect, self-concept is "negotiated" during early adolescence. It is during this developmental period that intellectual changes make it possible for students to think about thinking. The most powerful implication of this ability is a newfound ability for introspection. For the first time in their lives, young adolescents can think about who they are in functional ways. Everyone they meet is affected by everything they do and their views of themselves. Self-concept first emerges as a "global" construct. That is, students see themselves as able or unable, responsible or irresponsible, valuable or worthless. Only in later adolescence do their views of themselves begin to differentiate to include situations and specific dimensions of strength or weakness.

STUDENT: *I worry about getting an F on a test or forgetting an answer when the teacher calls on me. Another thing I worry about is having a boyfriend. My sister is real pretty and boys call her on the phone all the time. Boys don't like me cause I'm not tall. If a boy says something to me I never have anything to say back until he leaves and then it is too late.* (Female, age 12, 8th grade)

STUDENT: *I bumped into a teacher at school one day and made her spill some of her drink on herself and she jumped down my throat.* (Female, age 13, 9th grade)

A useful analogy for self-concept is the "Poker Chip Theory" suggested by Canfield and Wells (1976). They suggest that each student enters each class with a self-concept that is like a stack of chips. Some have had successful experiences in the past and enter with big stacks of chips. Others have been less successful and enter with small stacks. As in a poker game, the students with the larger stacks can afford to take chances and try new experiences. Those students who feel they have only a few chips left are not likely to take risks unless they can see a "sure thing." The ways in which teachers respond to students help them increase or decrease their stacks of chips.

The big lie

Perhaps the most powerful risk of early adolescence is the "big lie." The big lie told virtually to all young people is that they are inadequate because they are different. The lie is an inevitable part of childhood. It occurs when parents and teachers correct children. The media communicates it when "perfect" and not so "perfect" role models are projected into our homes through television programs and commercials. (Van Hoose, 1983; Giroux, 1996). It is reinforced by the inevitable tendency to compare the behavior of

49

one young person to others. The big lie reaches its greatest strength for young adolescents around the age of 12. It is during this time that middle level students compare themselves to others in almost every dimension of their development. Unfortunately, the inevitable conclusion they draw from their comparisons is that they are different, don't measure up, and therefore are inadequate. At this point, they come to believe the big lie. Zimmerman, Copeland, Shope, and Dielman's (1997) longitudinal study of adolescent self-esteem from grades six to ten reports that students in the decreasing self-esteem group had the greatest drop in grades six to eight thus supporting the concept of the "big lie." Though the extent and intensity of the sense of inadequacy varies, it is our contention that it occurs or has occurred in virtually everyone (including the readers of this book). Those young adolescents who have the greatest personal strength work their way through the big lie sooner and suffer less in the process. Those with less ego strength may spend the rest of their adolescent years as well as adulthood trying to come to terms with this message.

As young adolescents come to perceive themselves as inadequate, they develop patterns of behavior to attend to the perceived inadequacy. These coping behaviors are attempts at compensating for "flaws" or denying that "flaws" exist in themselves. One young person may become a fierce competitor in a sport. Another may become a perfectionist in academics. A third may direct all energies toward being the most popular. Some middle level students attempt to deny their inadequacies by not speaking out in class (so they cannot be told they are wrong) or by becoming a physical bully so no one can overtly reject them socially. In more destructive forms, a young adolescent may resort to drugs, avoid health care, or engage in other risk taking behaviors to avoid dealing with a painful reality (Van Hoose, 1991; Fraser, 1996; Farmer, Farmer, & Gut, 1999; Ford, Bearman, & Moody, 1999; O'Dea & Abraham, 1999).

 STUDENT: *In 6th and 7th grade I was afraid of the older boys. They liked to push us around. There was this little guy who was the gym assistant and he pushed us around the most.* (Male, age 13, 8th grade)

50

Many pass through these challenging years, and by the time they reach late adolescence, they let go of the big lie and embrace a view of themselves as competent persons. Unfortunately, some do not work through this sense of inadequacy and carry it with them for the rest of their lives. Their sense of inadequacy may affect their professional behavior as well as their personal behavior. The fierce competitor often rises to high levels in areas such as business, education, and politics and uses the power of executive positions to compensate for inadequacy. Their personal lives may also be affected in that their sense of inadequacy may be expressed in ways such as an inability to experience intimacy or demonstrate love for another in an intimate way. This type of inability reaffirms the sense of inadequacy and creates a pressure to compensate even more or leads to a need for professional help in dealing with their feelings about self.

Most of us feel less adequate in some ways. But, if we have come to terms with the big lie, we see our value as a person. We come to realize that we are indeed different – and that's just fine! But, until we reach that point, we will tend to try to compensate or deny our "perceived" inadequacies – and we will be unhappy. We say *perceived* because being different is not being less worthwhile. However, the big lie is so seductive because it reaches its greatest potency at a time when young people do not, above all else, want to be perceived as different, but can plainly see the evidence that they are so different. What, then, can we do to help young adolescents through this rather stormy set of challenges?

First, we can tell them about the big lie. We can convey that it's out there, lurking seductively, waiting to entice them into a sense of inadequacy. Second, we can convey the idea that they do not have to buy into this type of mind-set. They do not have to believe in the lie. Third, we can inform them that the lie is based on *perceived* differences between themselves and others. They need to know that whether they want to be different or not, they are at the stage of life when the differences are greater than at any other time in life. It is their right to decide that being bigger or smaller physically, being more talented or less talented in a sport or an academic area, being perceived as "better" looking or less attractive, doesn't have to cause them to decide that they are less worthwhile or less adequate. The differences are there, and we just need to accept them using our talents as best we can. Fourth, we can help young adolescents separate their behaviors from who they are. Parents and teachers have every right to expect appropriate behavior and hold young people accountable for their behavior. But, adults should deal with the behavior, not attack the character of a young person. Young adolescents need to begin to separate their behavior from their value as a person. Fifth, as professional helpers, we can concentrate on being as professionally and personally affirming and inviting as is appropriate and possible. This last statement requires some elaboration. There are certain behaviors that are personally affirming. If these are cultivated, youngsters will be much more effective in attending to the big lie and so much more likely to be freed up to

be the best that they can be academically as well as intellectually, socially, and personally.

One additional benefit to understanding the big lie is that it can help educators function more effectively since we can understand ourselves and the behavior of other adults. If a residue of the big lie still resides in us, then we need to come to terms with our own tendencies to be compulsive, or to be a perfectionist, or to expect that we are always right. We

Mastering an instrument and learning to read music advance intellectual development.

can also relate more effectively to colleagues, administrators, and parents who may be trying, through their behavior, to compensate for their own sense of inadequacy.

The big lie exists and can have tragic effects if not checked. If believed, it will cause young adolescents to direct most of their energies toward resolving it and can cause much unhappiness in the process. But it must be addressed so that young adolescents can establish equilibrium and a sense of well-being in their lives. It is our obligation to assist them in dealing with this major developmental challenge. If we help middle level students work through their sense of inadequacy, they will become happy, self-sufficient, productive, contributing adults in our society.

A sense of autonomy

Because young adolescents are in a transitional stage between childhood and late adolescence, they vacillate in their behaviors from being childlike to being more like adults. Larson, Richards, Meneta, and Duckett's (1996) study of adolescents' daily interactions with their families concludes that fifth graders who spent an average of 35 percent of their day with family see that time decrease in the eighth grade to only 14 percent of their day. The shifts in behavior are motivated not only by external indicators of the turmoil going on inside young adolescents, but in addition, by an increase in opportunities and pulls for adolescent experiences outside the family. These behaviors resonate throughout the school day. At times, young adolescents may want to be completely independent and think that they can undertake a task and complete it rather easily. For example, a teacher can explain the nature and use of adverbs and the students clearly see that it is easy for the teacher so it will be easy for them. They have no questions, and they can certainly apply the concepts just taught. Then, when asked to work on a few simple exercises, they storm the teacher for guidance. They thought they knew quite well, thank you, but found that they just couldn't do what was expected. They shift, in a heartbeat, from independence to dependence.

STUDENT: *Some of the teachers are great too. Notice I said SOME. I think the best teachers let you talk with each other sometimes, maybe when we are working in groups. These teachers also talk with us in class. Sometimes they talk to us about things that are not in our lessons and sometimes they talk with us about the lessons. You can talk about different things other than school subjects. I feel relaxed with these teachers. We trust each other.*

They seem to trust us and we trust them back. If you think they graded your paper wrong, they will give you a chance to come up and talk to them about it and we are not afraid of them. (Male, age 13, 9th grade)

It is also common for middle level students to ask teachers or parents for ideas about how to proceed on an experiment, what to say in a social situation, or what to wear, and then promptly reject whatever is suggested. They want adult input but also want to be able to accept it or reject it on their own terms. This move from dependence to independence often causes an adult to become frustrated, irritated, and at times, experience indigestion or heartburn.

These same young people may press to stay out later with friends at night, but may be afraid of the dark and want to leave the light on when going to bed. They may be willing to work hard at some tasks when they can clearly see immediate benefits, but may be very reluctant to apply themselves to tasks that supposedly pay off in the distant future when they can't see the tangible benefits here and now. These vacillations from childish to adult-like behavior are natural, and if teachers and parents keep this in mind, they will be less disappointed when they experience the certain-to-come unevenness in young adolescent behavior.

The Quality of Relationships with Peers and Adults

Any observer of middle school students will tell you that adolescents seem to be holding a number of identities concurrently. Depending on the situation and the value of the relationship, adolescents seem proficient in being able to adapt. Teachers often complain that parents will tell them that their child is an "angel" at home. This is the same child who can be disrespectful in class and sometimes treats peers with disdain. What causes adolescents to appear as if they have multiple personalities?

Relationships with peers

The web of social contacts and interactions experienced by middle level students is intricate, involves an extensive amount of time to sustain, and has a potent impact on the way young people think, feel, and act. The academic achievements of young adolescents may rise or fall due to the perceived quality of their social lives. If they feel rejected, they may invest an inordinate amount of time and energy on social matters to compensate for their sense of inadequacy. That leaves less time for academic concerns. If they feel accepted by peers, young adolescents are much more likely to apply themselves to academic work.

 STUDENT: *The best thing about my school is the teachers and my friends. Our teachers are real neat and they like us a lot, well most of them do. I would not want to go to another school because it would be hard to get to know new people. Here I know where everything is and I know the teachers' names and which ones are nice and which ones are mean. Sixth grade was fun because I learned a lot and got to see my friends.* (Female, age 11, 7th grade)

Acceptance by friends and others who are the same age is a central concern in the lives of young adolescents. In the extreme, a young person may be willing to commit acts of violence, take drugs, become sexually precocious, or be dependent on alcohol to be accepted by peers. More commonly, middle level students may be willing to be cruel to others, may deliberately make fun of others who are different from them, or may take risks like hassling teachers to be more accepted by their peers. Peers play an important role in adolescents' forming self-identity; social, academic and political attitudes; relationships with parents and other adults, and relationships with other peers (Hoge, 1999).

Those belonging to social groups cling to the security of that group to the point that they yield some of their own individuality and even behave in ways that run counter to the way they actually think and feel to maintain group membership. Those who do not belong to "premier" groups form their own sub-groups for support. These may be lower status groups, but they still help the members sustain themselves through a very "rocky" period of life. Peer groups often take over the supportive roles traditionally found in a family. The Carnegie Council on Adolescent Development (1989) report states that peer support may be especially important for those whose parents are emotionally distant, harshly critical, or casually neglectful.

 STUDENT: *At the beginning of the year, I always worry about having friends and if I will have anyone to sit with on the bus and at lunch. Sometimes I wish I were more like my sister cause everyone likes her and she can always think of things to say.*
(Female, age 12, 8th grade)

We should be concerned about those who are the isolates. They are not typically isolates by choice. Rather, they are rejected because they don't meet "appearance" standards or don't understand the proper meaning of hygiene. They smell or they act differently – they are "weird," "dumb," or "air-heads." Or they dress differently because they are poor, or they don't receive proper guidance on how to dress. The result is that they are ridiculed, harassed, and humiliated. These "isolates" are often the ones most disconnected with school, thus potentially at risk for dropping out (Scales, 1996). Most young adolescents are not mature enough to withstand peer pressure, and they do what they believe will please their friends. Unfortunately, most young people are hurt in one way or another in the process. While they may be members of one group, they are not part of other groups, or they may have no group membership. Most young adolescents have been the target for ridicule and hurt at some point; for these reasons, it is not a consistently happy time of life for many of them. Teachers need to be aware that the dramatic mood fluctuations are due, in part, to the success or lack thereof that young adolescents experience in their quest for peer acceptance.

Relationships with family.
All of us know about and may have experienced in some way the changes in family life that have occurred in contemporary society. It is certainly true that an increasing number of young adolescents come from homes that do not contain the birth parents. Rather, an increasing number of middle level students come from single parent homes, homes with one step-parent and

one original parent, or from homes headed by a relative (i.e., aunt, uncle, grandparent) but neither parent. Many students, of course, still come from homes where both original parents reside, but there are more combinations of families than ever before. Irrespective of whether this condition is good or bad – it just is.

Student-led conferences encourage students to assume responsibility.

A supportive, loving home life may exist in any of these settings. At the same time, a destructive environment may exist as well. A major point to keep in mind is that within each home, all the members (mother, father, children, grandparents, or others) have their own histories, characteristics, stresses, and needs (Hoge, 1999). When taking this complexity of family members into consideration, remember that it is not family composition that makes the difference; rather, it is the quality of life in the home (Van Hoose & Legrand, 2000). It may be more difficult for single parents, or caretakers who are not parents to create and sustain the most desirable home environment for young adolescents, but many invest the time and energy to do so. It is time to debunk the "myth" about children from "broken" homes and embrace a more enlightened perspective. *Broken* is a very poor word choice; for as one of our friends following a divorce remarked, "My home used to be 'broken.' Now it is fixed." Young adolescents can come from a wide range of family structures and be well-adjusted, happy, and contributing members of society.

At the same time, it has to be recognized that family allegiances universally become somewhat shaky during early adolescence. In the quest for maturity, middle level students push against established limits. These limits constitute what can be watched on television, what can and cannot be done to a younger brother or sister, how long the telephone can be tied up, what they can and cannot wear, where they can go, and how late they can stay out. The tendency of adolescents to push limits to a moderate extent is important and appropriate in establishing a true and effective identity (Newcomb, 1996). Yet these and other issues can become battlegrounds between parents and young adolescents. Who is in charge often becomes more important than the immediate issue. Young adolescents want the privileges of adults and the freedom to do whatever they want. Because they lack the maturity to handle a number of these privileges, parents draw the line and say "no."

Parents not only have the right to set limits, they have a responsibility to set and enforce them. Yet young adolescents behave as though it is their sacred right to challenge these limits. When parents do what they should do, students will do what comes naturally; they will resist, plead, confront, sulk a little, and manipulate reality ("everyone else gets to go") to have their way. These confrontations are what make family allegiances appear shaky. Both parents and young adolescents may become angry (even furious), frustrated, stressed out, and a bit resentful at times. The only consolation to these numerous interactions that occur with varying intensity between most parents and young adolescents who care about each other is that both survive and typically arrive at a more harmonious relationship as young adolescents mature. Disagreements and fighting (not the physical type) are inevitable to establish who is in control.

We worry much more about the many young adolescents who are not given proper direction and supervision, and as a result, do not experience the appropriate conflict at home. These are the young people who may go far beyond the accepted limits and engage in personally destructive behaviors (Scaramella, Conger, Simons, & Whitebeck, 1998). Papini's (1994) review of research related to family structure and adolescent identity formation

58

concluded that adolescents whose family systems encourage open patterns of communication and flexible adaptability should be better equipped to explore and make commitments to life alternatives than adolescents from family systems characterized by closedness and rigidity.

In sum, if parents, caretakers, or teachers love young adolescents, they will give them only as much freedom as they can responsibly handle. They will set reasonable limits and sensitively enforce them. Though young adolescents push at the limits, they still need them and expect them, and in the long run, may even appreciate them because such limits say that someone cares.

Implications: Finding Ways
to Provide Security, Success, Support

Personal needs can be summarized with three words: *security, support,* and *success.* While young adolescents often seem self-assured, interviews and survey responses indicate that most of them need to *feel secure.* Among the top fears they often list are the loss of a parent, nuclear war, and disease. As children, they may have known these fears, but as adolescents, they may dwell on them. Even when they manage to put such fears in perspective, their thoughts reveal a mixture of optimism and anxiety. The following "bio-poem" written by an eighth grader illustrates this phenomenon – a combination of child-like joy and adult-like fears.

Janet, Daughter of Mr. and Mrs. Smith

Cheerful, friendly, outgoing, musical,
Daughter of Mr. & Mrs. Donald Smith,
Likes Backstreet Boys, summer,
Playing sports,
Feels good around people, happy most,
Of the time, sad when it rains,
Fears going new places, meeting new
People, death,
Would like to see the world in peace
Smiling faces all the time,
Backstreet Boys in person.
Resident of Winston-Salem.

The need for security has grown even more pronounced with the cultural changes of recent decades. There was a time when many young adolescents felt the presence of a "safety net" composed of family, extended family, friends, and community. Even though they experienced the uncertainties caused by the passage into adulthood, they were aware of the security provided by parents, siblings, and relatives, and a familiar community where people knew them and cared for them. This sense of relational security extends into an individual's perception of happiness. Magen's (1998) cross-cultural study on adolescents' perception of happiness found that adolescents experience joy from relationships with peers and family members. These experiences were centered on feelings of being trusted. While many young adolescents may feel this "safety net" as one factor in the experience of happiness, many others have felt the anxieties of disrupted homes and a more "mobile" society. They may have attended several schools, lived in several neighborhoods, or never really known grandparents or an extended family. These factors may accentuate the loneliness of adolescence and the need for as secure an environment as possible.

A related need is *support*. As they try to define their own identity and begin to break away from their parents, most young adolescents need to establish close relationships with adults who are not their parents. Teachers usually fill this role.

STUDENT: *Everybody thinks Coach K. is the greatest teacher and coach. He can explain games in a way that you really know how to play them and he chooses games that are really fun to play. Sometimes, like in badminton, he'd take on the whole class. He'd be on one side and we'd all be on the other. He had this way of talking that made you know you were all right. He also had a way of picking on the goofiest guy in the class. We'd say that if Coach K. picked on you that meant he liked you. Sometimes, I'd wish that Coach K. would pick on me.*

(Male, age 14, 8th grade)

Teachers often observe this need for support when students begin to "hang around" their classrooms before or after school for no apparent reason. Sometimes, students just want to talk – about anything. They want to talk about their interests and adventures, tell bad jokes, or just sit and listen to others. Some students become very close to their scout leaders, coaches, or Sunday school teachers for the same reason. They want to find adults who will accept them and have "adult" conversations. They often find it easier to talk with a teacher than with their parents, especially about the changes in their lives and how they feel about them. This need for *support* is more than acceptance. It is a need to feel a part of the world of adults.

> INTERVIEWER: *Now, I want you to think about the teacher you like the least and describe that teacher for me.*
>
> STUDENT: *She was pretty mean. Anytime we had something to do, she'd just tell you to do it, no questions asked or answered. She wouldn't let you go see the guidance counselor if you had a problem. She went over some of the work, but most of it you had to get on your own.*
>
> INTERVIEWER: *Would this teacher listen to your problems, or did you ever feel like going to her with your problems?*
>
> STUDENT: *No, I saw what happened to the other kids. They went to the office for just asking one little question.* (Female, age 14, 9th grade)

In addition to security and support, young adolescents need *success*. As suggested throughout this book, they need to feel valuable, able, and responsible. Successful academic and social experiences nurture self-concept (Jarvinen & Nicholls, 1996). When they feel accepted by their teachers and peers, they are more likely to do well in school. Even more powerful in determining achievement is how they feel about themselves as learners. It has long been known that one of the best predictors of academic achievement is self-concept. Children who finish first grade convinced that they can read well and are successful are far more likely to be good readers in the sixth grade than those who feel they are poor readers. We believe that the same is true of every subject. The need for success in the middle grades is especially acute, however. The longitudinal study on student motivation conducted by Eccles and associates (1993) documents the "turn off syndrome" that characterizes some students' experiences in middle grades. In an intensive study of over 2500 students from middle and lower middle socioeconomic communities, the researchers found that students' self-esteem and confidence in their abilites (academic and social) decreased when they transitioned into middle school. They concluded

> The decline in motivation often assumed to be characteristic of the early adolescence period are less a consequence of students' developmental stage than of a mismatch between students' needs and the opportunities afforded them in a traditional middle school. (p. 567)

Middle level teachers can have tremendous influence in fostering a student's sense of "success." Strahan (1989, 1997) and Strahan & Strahan's (1988) studies of student perception of school have underscored the importance of helping students see themselves as valuable, able, and responsible. In the classes where students learn self-control and self-discipline, they are "connected" with either the teacher or the subject matter. Van Hoose (1989, 1991) and Van Hoose and LeGrand (2000) described an exemplary program that focused on the most challenging population of students in any school (the disconnected and high at-risk students) and succeeded in reconnecting these students to school. The staff there believed that the barriers to academic success were embedded primarily in social and emotional concerns, and once these barriers are removed, students can focus more fully on academics.

 STUDENT: *I don't like it when teachers are rude to kids because it can hurt your feelings. You know sometimes a kid says something real dumb and the teacher gets all mad. [How do you know she is mad?] You know, she kind of holds her breath, and rolls*

her eyes like this... Nobody has done that to me yet, but some-
times I am afraid they might. I don't like it when kids get in
trouble because when the teacher yells it gives me a headache.
Even if kids are bad, the teacher shouldn't yell because everyone
can hear it. I think they should take them in the hall or to the
office so everyone doesn't get in trouble.

(Female, age 11, 7th grade)

Conclusion

Young adolescents form a healthy sense of identify when they can address their needs for competence, autonomy, and social support.

In spite of their apparent buoyancy, they are fragile, perhaps more fragile than at any other time in their lives. As we will affirm in the last chapter, the most successful schools and the most successful teachers in the middle grades are those who meet young adolescents' needs for security, support, and success in a proactive manner. ◑

5. Promoting Harmony in the Middle Grades Through School Practices

A recent report, *Turning Points 2000* (Jackson & Davis, 2000) draws on the lessons learned from several national middle grades improvement efforts and on the latest research. *Turning Points 2000* is an in-depth examination of how to improve middle grades education, providing much more "flesh on the bone" than the original. *Turning Points 2000* builds on the premise of the eight original recommendations listed below, but the reordered seven recommendations reflect what we have learned in the decade since the original report in 1989. The focus of the current recommendations is curriculum, instruction, and assessment; and the authors place heavy emphasis on these elements as "design" elements, each working together to create a successful middle level school. *Turning Points 2000* reaffirms the purposes of middle grades schools.

> Let us be clear. The main purpose of middle grades education is to promote young adolescents' intellectual development. ....Closely related goals are to help all students develop the capacity to lead healthful lives, physically and mentally; to become caring, compassionate; and tolerant individuals; to become active, contributing citizens of the United States and the world. (pp. 10-11)

As stated earlier, the thesis of this book is that successful middle schools are those truly designed to meet the needs of young adolescents. In the same manner, successful teachers are those who address these needs proactively. Recent major reports on effective middle schools provide a number of insights into how successful schools and teachers meet the needs of their students.

Felner and his colleagues completed a series of studies on the impact of "the middle school concept." Data gathered over three years from 97 middle schools show that the more successful schools have been in implementing the recommendations from *Turning Points* (1989), the more successful students have been on measures of achievement and well-being (Felner et al., 1997). More specifically, the most successful schools have shown greater progress in implementing these original *Turning Points* recommendations.

- Create small communities for learning
- Teach a core academic program
- Ensure success for all students
- Empower teachers and administrators to make decisions
- Staff middle grades schools with teachers who are experts at teaching young adolescents
- Improve academic performance through fostering the health and fitness of young adolescents
- Reengage families in the education of young adolescents
- Connect schools with communities (Carnegie Council on Adolescent Development, 1989)

Implementing these recommendations provides educational opportunities that address the developmental needs of young adolescents. Successful schools are thus "caring" schools and encourage students and teachers to succeed in a myriad of ways that stem from commitment.

In *Turning Points 2000: Educating Adolescents in the 21st Century* (2000), Jackson and Davis present a synthesis of research that enriches the recommendations of the original *Turning Points* (1989) report. They note that "significant progress has been made in the journey to provide young adolescents with a developmentally responsive education" (p. 5). Even so, they conclude that "we are only halfway up the mountain with the most important and perhaps most difficult part of the climb remaining" (p. 5). Jackson and Davis insist that the challenge middle level educators face in the 21st century is to apply what we have learned to meeting the needs of "schools serving the highest concentrations of low-performing students" (p. 5). This challenge framed the "Turning Points model" that they delineate, beginning with one overarching goal, "ensuring success for every student" (p. 23).

An attractive environment helps to promote harmony in a school.

These reports point out that the process of becoming a more successful school begins with an understanding of young adolescents and an appreciation of their unique needs. Our studies support this position. As we have interacted with hundreds of different teachers in a wide variety of middle schools, we have identified a number of specific school practices that promote either harmony or discord in relationship to student needs. In the pages that follow, we present an overview of these harmonious and discordant practices as they relate to categories of student needs. We have organized these practices according to the constructs of the developmental assets (Benson, Galbraith, & Espeland, 1998) outlined in Chapter One.

For each category of assets, we describe middle level practices that promote "harmony" and others that create disharmony or "discord." We then illustrate one "featured performance" in each category. Just as an orchestra sometimes spotlights a particular instrument or performer, these featured performances represent exemplary practices that characterize harmony in action.

1. Support

Strong support from caring adults undergirds the full range of developmental needs. Rapid rates of sexual and other physical changes can make young adolescents vulnerable to new feelings and personal risk. Caring adults can enhance both physical and psychological safety. Emotional and social changes can create a sense of upheaval. Caring adults can provide a sense of security. Intellectual changes can provoke soul-searching and new levels of inquiry. Caring adults can provide guidance and encouragement. All of these types of support are necessary to create a climate for growth.

D – **the aloof staff:** In some schools we have visited we rarely saw teachers talking with students before school or between classes. Teachers congregated in the lounge or stayed to themselves. In one extreme situation, we observed a teacher who grabbed a student by the neck and stood him against the lockers because he happened to walk between two teachers who were talking. In a different school, a student provided another discordant note:

> STUDENT: *I would also get rid of the hateful school secretary. There is one at my school that the kids call the dragon lady. She will snap your head off if you have to go into the office for any reason. I hate to have to go in there with a note from home if I have to go the doctor or somewhere. She hates kids.*
>
> (Male, age 13, 8th grade)

H – **the student-centered staff:** Teachers in successful schools find opportunities to talk with students outside of class. We have seen teachers seated on their desks surrounded by students before homeroom or advisory begins. We have seen them walking, eating lunch, playing basketball or chess with students, and singing songs together. One school we visited schedules weekend outings several times each year. These outings are not only field trips, but social events as well, a chance for any student who wishes to take part in the community of the school. One student conveys the following example of harmony.

STUDENT: *Miss T. has a great sense of humor. She doesn't mind if you laugh as long as it is not at someone else. You can't laugh though when she is teaching something new, then she is real serious cause she knows it is important. You can tell Miss T. really likes us cause she is always asking us what we think about certain things. You can go to her if you have a problem with a friend or something and she won't tell anyone. She understands that things are hard sometimes and that some days are just bad. If she gets mad at you for something she doesn't stay mad for long. She will talk to you and then be nice again. Nobody wants to make Miss T. mad cause she is real nice to everybody.* (Female, age 12, 8th grade)

Featured Performance
A "safety net" of services

Successful middle-level schools anticipate students' needs for support and provide a connected set of services in the areas of health, wellness, family, peers, and academics. We use the analogy of a "safety net" to describe these connected sets of services. Like a safety net, these services are there to catch students when they may "fall" into any potential risk area. While the strands in the net may vary from school to school, what matters most is that the net is there, that it is inspected often, and that when anyone needs it, caring adults are there to hold it in place.

---

2. Empowerment

We have characterized early adolescence as a time of physical changes and energetic activity, a time when many students literally "bounce" down hallways and off each other. Taps, pokes, and occasional hugs or punches are ways young adolescents define themselves and each other. We have suggested that "sitting still" is not only difficult but sometimes painful as well. These outward signals show us that young adolescents want to influence their physical environment and remind us that they

69

want to influence their social and psychological environments as well. Just as some schools seem to try to "fight" students needs for attention and socialization, some schools seem to try to "strait-jacket" students' needs for physical activity. Successful schools, once again, find ways to address this need.

D – **the fifty-minute lecture:** It is very difficult for most adults to sit and listen for fifty-minutes – even to a captivating speaker. Teachers who expect their students to stay tuned to a lecture or other passive activity for forty to fifty minutes have a difficult time holding their audience. The minuscule amount of exercise that may be provided by notetaking rarely offsets the demands of staying seated for a single activity for an entire class period.

H – **project options:** By providing options for students to demonstrate their understanding of concepts, successful teachers build movement into their lessons and give students choices about ways to show their comprehension. Some students may choose to draw; others may prefer to construct a model, present a skit, write a poem, or use music. These project options create opportunities for variety and responsible decision-making.

Featured Performance
Intramural sports programs

Many of the most successful middle schools emphasize intramural sports programs that encourage everyone to participate. A wide range of choices is offered and supervised school facilities are available before and after the school day. One of our successful schools plans an intramural sports program that takes place during the school day, so every student in the school can play on a team. No one is excluded because of bus rides or other after-school activities.

---

3. Boundaries and expectations

While we have attempted throughout to describe the "unpredictability" of early adolescence, we have also suggested that middle school students need routine, limits, and structure.

Even though students need to test limits and assert their independence, they also need to know what to expect and the consequences for their actions. The concept of a circle is often used to characterize successful discipline, for example. When students know where the circle is and what happens when they try to step outside, they spend less time testing limits. When the lines of the circle keep changing or they have to guess how big the circle is, they are more likely to "play games." In successful schools, limits are clear but unobtrusive and the school day is structured but not regimented. One student reflects on this need.

> STUDENT: *I also like the good discipline system we have in our school. The principal tells us the rules at the beginning of every school year and then again during the rest of the year. If things are not going smoothly at our school and kids are getting rowdy, he will call an assembly, tell us he is not happy with the situation, and go over the rules again with us. We have fair rules at our school. I don't know who made them up because they were there when I got there, but they are very fair. Some of the rules are about no fighting and being on time. The classroom teachers make their own rules about gum chewing.* (Male, age 13, 8th grade)

D – **the prison lunchroom:** In several schools we have visited, students have assigned seats in the cafeteria. In some instances, they even have "silent lunch." One principal said to us, "Isn't it fantastic how quiet our lunchroom is?" One of these schools has "silent homeroom" and "silent bus zone" as well.

> INTERVIEWER'S COMMENT: *Students put friends at the top of the most enjoyable category, with field trips a distant second. It is not surprising that students do not enjoy lunch, since they have assigned tables where they must sit while the assistant principal patrols the cafeteria.*

H – **the friendly (but louder) lunchroom:** Successful schools provide a cafeteria setting that promotes friendly conversation. One school has a salad bar made from an old car. Several provide picnic tables for use in fair weather. In one school, students may eat at various stations throughout the building.

71

Featured Performance
A "low card" approach to discipline

In *Positive Discipline - A Pocketful of Ideas,* Purkey
and Strahan (1986) describe a "low card approach" to
discipline. When a player in a card game has to
decide which card to play, he or she most often
wants to take a trick "as cheaply as possible." It
makes little sense to play an ace when a lower card
would win as well. Similarly, a teacher wants to
invite good discipline with as little energy and time
expended as possible (p. 20). Students are encour-
aged to stay on task most effectively when a teacher
monitors behavior and sends corrective signals in the
most unobtrusive way possible. A "low card" sequence for "talking during directions" might be as
follows.

• raising eyebrows in an inquisitive fashion
• staring politely (steady gaze)
• pausing briefly while continuing to stare
• moving closer to the student while continuing to
  talk
• gently placing a hand on the students shoulder
  while continuing directions
• using the student's name as part of the directions
• asking the student by name to listen to directions
                                                (p. 20)

"Low card" approaches provide structure without
promoting disruption. Students learn limits without
automatically being placed "on stage." In the sequence above, the teacher does not stop giving
directions to directly address misbehavior until he or
she has taken seven other steps first. As one teacher
suggested, "As soon as I stop what I am teaching to
confront a misbehaving student, it's 'show time' and
everyone stops learning to see the show."

4. Constructive use of time

In our descriptions and vignettes, we have tried to portray some of the richness of this developmental period. We find middle grades students are capable of wonderful insights that appear most often when they are nurtured rather than left to chance. Successful teachers find ways to cultivate ideas rather than just present them.

$\mathcal{D}$ – **"Open your books, read Chapter 7, and answer the questions."** One of the least effective ways to teach is among the most commonly used. When teachers give assignments such as the one above, students are not motivated. Such assignments are very inefficient, because students have little sense of purpose and tend to read mechanically. Most of them simply "look up the answers." They have no concrete experiences to serve as springboards to concepts. Studies of memory suggest that students will forget most of what they read under such conditions within 24 hours.

$\mathcal{H}$ – **Academic Learning Time (ALT):** Among the many findings to emerge from the Far West Lab studies in the 1970s was the distinction between time-on-task (busywork) and "Academic Learning Time" (ALT). Researchers discovered that the best measure of student learning was the time they spent engaged in tasks they viewed as meaningful and those they felt they could complete successfully. During reading time, for example, those students who have books they want to read and those who will spend their time actually reading them will improve their reading. If a student reads actively for 20 minutes of a 30-minute block of time, he/she will accumulate twenty minutes of Academic Learning Time. If a student spends twenty-five minutes looking for a book or "turning pages" and only five minutes reading, he accumulates only five minutes of ALT. Over the course of a school year, the amount of ALT that a teacher encourages is directly related to how much students learn.

Featured Performance
Hands-on/minds-on lessons

Successful teachers "build" concepts. They often
begin with opportunities for students to think about
what they already know about the topic and activities
that build motivation and set induction. For example,
one teacher we observed began a lesson on "balanc-
ing equations" with a discussion of balance. When
one student suggested that "you have to balance on a
balance beam," the teacher asked him to come to the
front of the class and demonstrate walking on a thin
line. She then asked students to describe what they
saw. Several students suggested that when he leaned
one way, he had to put his arm out the other way.
They defined "balance" as "evening things out." She
then used a balance scale and weights to demonstrate
a different type of balance. Students then defined
"balance" as keeping both sides even. At this point,
the teacher demonstrated how to balance several
equations. Students then generated a mathematical
definition. In this lesson, they did not start reading
and answering questions until they generated the
critical concept they needed for success.

PRACTICES THAT BUILD, OR WEAKEN *INTERNAL* ASSETS

1. Commitment to learning

Successful middle level schools provide students ongoing
support for developing self-discipline. One of the biggest transitions that occurs across the middle grades is the progression
toward greater responsibility for one's actions. The external
supports described above enhance the likelihood that the school
environment will further this transition. Internally, students need
to develop a stronger sense of self-motivation.

74

D – **busywork:** In some classrooms, pressures for account-ability result in more busywork. As pointed out throughout this book, young adolescents need to know the purpose of assignments and see them as meaningful if they are to learn from them. One of the most dramatic illustrations of busywork is provided in the movie *Teachers*. One of the teachers in that movie came to be known as "Ditto" because he used excessive seatwork. Even though Ditto had won his district's award for the most organized classroom, his students did nothing except seatwork. Ditto had his students so routinized that they distributed the dittos themselves while Ditto often slept at his desk. In this satirical film, he dies behind his newspaper one day and none of his students notice. Assuming he was asleep, they conducted business as usual.

H – **concentration activities:** In more productive class-rooms, students learn to monitor their own involvement and learning. One way to promote self-discipline is to offer recurring opportunities to reflect on levels of concentration. Almost any assignment can provide a context for the following types of questions.

1. To what extent does this task engage your thinking?
2. If you find that you concentrate well on this task, what is there about the task that encourages you to focus so well?
3. If your mind is wandering, what is there about this task that you find disengaging?
4. What are your most frequent obstacles to concentration?
5. When something seems boring or distracting, how can you try to re-focus your attention?
6. Does it help to think about the reasons for the assignment, the prospects for reward, the consequences of inattention?
7. How can your teachers, parents, or friends help you improve your concentration?

Featured Performance
Student-led conferences

While conferences between parents and teachers regarding student work have long been part of the school landscape, in recent years, a growing number of educators have realized that such conferences are much more meaningful when students take the lead. As Farber (1999) notes, this concept is growing in popularity because participating students show "long-lasting improvements in students' intellectual focus," and teachers report "less stress, fewer complaints, and better attendance on conference day" (p. 21). Student-led conferences follow a natural progression: students begin the meeting with their parent(s) or other adults by showing examples of their work, explain how they have evaluated these works with their teachers, and discuss goals for the next few months (p. 22). Such conferences require careful planning. Farber notes that the preparation process has many benefits in and of itself.

Such planning typically requires three to five class sessions and three major steps.

1. compiling and organizing work samples
2. reflecting on their successes and failures
3. practicing what they will say during the conference. (p. 22)

By encouraging students to select works that show a range of learning experiences, to assess their own progress, and to role-play the conference process, teachers promote commitment to learning. Students learn to take more responsibility for monitoring their own academic performance and gain confidence from taking the lead in reporting their progress (Kinney, Munroe, & Sessions, 2000).

2. Positive values

Part of learning self-discipline is understanding personal values. During the transition from childhood to adulthood, students naturally ask themselves many questions about their values. They try to sort through the messages they receive about what it means to be good, to care for others, and to take care of themselves. The adults in their lives play an essential role in this process.

D – **negative role models:** A superintendent invited one of the authors on a "walking tour" of a school that included visits to classrooms. One teacher told us that the reason this class was working at a more basic level in reading was that "all of these students are slow." She made this unsolicited comment in front of the students – and they heard it. This comment was insensitive and disrespectful. When adults model such destructive behavior, students are more likely to engage in behavior that is hurtful to each other.

H – **positive role models:**

STUDENT: *My homeroom teacher is my favorite teacher. She is always nice in the morning when you come in. On Mondays she always asks about our weekends and tells us what she and her husband did. She knows a lot about plants and has spider plants all over the classroom. One time she brought in an orange cactus. A boy accidentally knocked it off the cabinet and all the dirt went everywhere. He was really scared that he was going to get in trouble cause she likes plants and all but she just laughed and said it was her fault for putting it in someone's way. Then the boy laughed too and they cleaned it up. The next day she brought the cactus back in new dirt and got the boy to find a safe place for it. At the end of the year she gives her plants away.* (Female, age 12, 8th grade)

Featured Performance
Service learning

The concept of service has long been a part of middle level education. Over the years, teachers, administrators, and parents have worked with students to find ways they could contribute to their schools and communities. Scales (1999) reports that formal programs featuring service learning have grown more popular in recent years. His study of the impact of service learning on more than 1000 middle school students in three different programs shows that these experiences have positive benefits for students when such experiences meet three key conditions.

1. Students spend a significant amount of time engaged in service learning (more than 31 hours per year).
2. Students have opportunities to reflect on their experiences
3. Students feel such experiences are linked with their classes (p. 40).

Students who reported experiences that met these conditions.
- significantly improved in their sense of duty to others
- significantly increased their sense that they could make a difference when helping others
- maintained their sense that school provided developmental opportunities such as decision making and recognition from adults
- declined less than other students in their commitment to classwork
- improved somewhat in pursuing good grades(pp. 40-41).

His results confirm our observations that students form positive values when caring adults provide them systematic opportunities to care for their classmates and their communities.

3. Social competencies

As we have suggested, early adolescence can be a very fragile time for many students. Many young adolescents feel a heightened sense of anxiety about their academic, social, and athletic abilities. On the one hand, they want attention and recognition; on the other, they want to be part of a crowd. The types of attention and confirmation they receive in the school environment are especially important.

D – **the "star system":** In some schools, relatively few students receive the bulk of the attention and recognition; they are stars on the athletic teams, are selected to be cheerleaders, are elected to the student council and honor society, and in other ways are recognized. When it is time for the awards assembly, their names are called out repeatedly. Educators call this the "star system."

H – **a wide range of awards:** In more successful schools, many students receive some type of recognition. Some schools give varsity-type awards for all sorts of activities – academic achievement, involvement in drama, school service activities, and community service. Every student has a chance to be "spotlight student of the week" or to be interviewed for the school paper.

Participating in activities that have value in and of themselves creates a positive climate for learning.

Another way in which middle grades students differ from their elementary counterparts is the degree to which they need social interaction. While elementary students enjoy opportunities to talk and play, middle grades students must have time together. For some students school is the only time when they can be with their friends. All students look forward to whatever time they have to "catch up" or "hang out." Some schools try to fight this need. More successful schools find ways to integrate social and academic learning.

Featured Performance
Lessons that allow social interaction

Successful teachers find ways to allow students to talk with each other and teach concepts at the same time. An excellent example is a lesson we observed called "Pizza Hut Math." In a unit on decimals, the teacher divided the class into groups and gave students menus from Pizza Hut. Each group selected a waiter or waitress who recorded orders. Each student then ordered from the menu. Students added decimals to figure the bill, multiplied decimals to determine sales tax and the tip, and divided to determine each person's share. At the same time, they practiced the social skills of ordering from a menu and working together. Everyone enjoyed the lesson tremendously and sharpened math skills in an innovative fashion.

---

4. Positive identity

We have taken the position that the development of a positive self-concept may be the most important need of young adolescents. Physical, social, intellectual, and personal changes interact and create a kaleidoscopic situation out of which they try to determine who they are and how they relate to the "adult world." Some schools seem to ignore this powerful need for self-exploration. They simply offer students more of the same types of activities and experiences they have had in elementary school.

Successful schools, in contrast, find a variety of ways to address their students' needs for self-exploration.

D – **the factory model school day:** The school day can be much like an assembly line. Students "check in" to a homeroom that is little like a home, report quickly to their first class, jump and run at the sound of bells several times, perform a series of routine activities, stand in long lunch lines, return quickly after a few minutes to an afternoon of more of the same, and exit quickly when the final bell rings.

H – **exploratory learning opportunities:** In successful schools, students have choices. They participate in a variety of exploratory learning opportunities in enrichment programs and in their content classes. They have many opportunities to discuss their ideas and to select project options that allow them to express those ideas. Johnston (1985) reports that in one school, an art teacher has a large collection of "rejects," projects that students have started and then abandoned because they did not "fit." Sometimes other students take one of these and complete it. Whatever the outcome, no one has to complete a project for the sake of completing it.

Featured Performance
Adviser/advisee across the day

The purpose of advisory is to ensure that every student is well known by at least one adult in a middle level school (Carnegie Council on Adolescent Development, 1989). This can be done through planned, open-ended advisor/advisee sessions occurring in small groups. These discussions can promote self-understanding and understanding of others in a safe environment or "opportunity." Times can be structured to interact one-on-one on topics of interest and concern. These can be brief but meaningful interactions that can lead to lengthier discussions as needed (during an appropriate block of instruction or after school). Ideally, these touch points should occur on a daily basis. In this way, advisory becomes "A/A across the day" (Van Hoose, 1991).

A final word

Throughout this book we have identified and analyzed the developmental characteristics of young adolescents together with the challenges and opportunities these characteristics create for educators. We emphasized that teachers and other helping professionals can diminish the discord and enhance the harmony in the lives of middle grades students. We shared examples of some of the discord we have observed and marveled at the harmony we have witnessed. In our work with middle grades educators, we have encountered many dedicated professionals who are committed to nurturing positive experiences in their schools. We hope that this publication will encourage additional efforts on behalf of young adolescents and increase the likelihood of harmonious experiences in middle grades settings. ❧

When students work together they learn more and build personal relationships.

References

Amshler, D. H. (1999). Calcium intake in adolescents: An issue revisited. *Journal of School Health, 69,* 120-122.

Arnold, J., & Stevenson, C. (1998). *Teachers teaming handbook: A middle level planning guide.* New York: Teachers College Press.

Arth, A. (1992, November). *How to begin, revise, and continue to develop an excellent middle level program.* Presentation at the National Middle School Association Conference, Portland, OR.

Baker, S. S., & Cochrane, W. J. (1999). Calcium requirements of infants, children, and adolescents. *Pediatrics, 104,* 1152-1157.

Balk, D. E. (1995). *Adolescent development: Early through late adolescence.* Pacific Grove, CA: Brooks Grove Publishing.

Benson, P. L., Galbraith, J., & Espeland, P. (1998). *What kids need to succeed.* Minneapolis, MN: Free Spirit Publishing, Inc.

Canfield, J., & Wells, H. C. (1976). *100 ways to enhance self-concept in the classroom.* Englewood Cliffs, NJ: Prentice-Hall.

Carnegie Council on Adolescent Development. (1989). *Turning points; Preparing American youth for the 21st century.* New York: Carnegie Corporation.

Carnegie Council on Adolescent Development. (1995). *Great transitions: Preparing adolescents for a new century.* New York: Carnegie Corp.

Centers for Disease Control. (2000, May). Data sources and method. Retrieved May 2000 from the World Wide Web: http:www.cdc.gov./

Csikszentmihalyi, M. (1989). The dynamics of intrinsic motivation: a study of adolescents. *Research on Motivation in Education, Volume 3,* 45-71.

Csikszentmihalyi, M. (1990). Literacy and intrinsic motivation. *Daedalus, 119* (2), 115-140.

Eccles, J. S., Wigfield, A., Midgley, C., Reuman, D., MacIver, D., & Feldlaufer, H. (1993). Negative effects of traditional middle schools on students' motivation. *The Elementary School Journal, 93,* 553-574.

Elkind, D. (1967). Egocentrism in adolescence. *Child development, 38,* 1025-1034.

Erickson, E. H. (1968). *Identity: Youth and crisis.* New York: Norton.

Farber, P. (1999). Speak up: Student-led conference is a real conversation piece. *Middle Ground, 2* (4), 20-24.

Farmer, T. W., Farmer, E. M. Z., & Gut, D. M. (1999). Implications of social development research for school-based interventions for aggressive youth with EBD. *Journal of Emotional and Behavioral Disorders, 7,* 130-137.

Federal Interagency Forum on Child and Family Statistics. (1999). *America's children: Key indicators of well-being.* Washington, D.C.: Author.

Felner, R.D., Jackson, A.W., Kasak, D., Mulhall, P., Brand, S. & Flowers, N. (1997). The impact of school reform for the middle school years. *Phi Delta Kappan, 78* (7) 528-532, 541-550.

Ford, C., Bearman, P., & Moody, J. (1999). Foregone healthcare among adolescents. *Journal of the American Medical Association, 282,* 2227-2237.

Forney, M. S., Forney, P. D., & Van Hoose, J. (1985). The causes of alcohol abuse by young adolescents. *Middle school research: Selected studies.* Columbus, OH: National Middle School Association.

Fraser, M. W. (1996). Aggressive behavior in childhood and early adolescence: An ecological-developmental perspective on youth violence. *Social Work, 41,* 347-362.

Gardner, H. (1983). *Frames of mind: The theory of multiple intelligences.* New York: Basic Books.

Gardner, H. (1995). Reflections on multiple intelligences: Myths and messages. *Phi Delta Kappan, 77* (4), 200-209.

Gardner, H., & Hatch, T. (1989). Multiple intelligences go to school. *Educational Researcher, 18* (8), 4-10.

Giroux, H. A. (1996). *Fugitive cultures: Race violence and youth.* New York: Routledge.

Glasser, W. (1986). *Control theory in the classroom.* New York: Harper and Row.

Goleman, D. (1995). *Emotional intelligence.* New York: Bantam Books.

Hinton, S. E. (1967). *The outsiders.* New York: Dell Publishing Co., Inc.

Hockenberry-Eaton, M., & Richman, M. J. (1996). Mother and adolescent knowledge of sexual development: The effects of gender, age and sexual experience. *Adolescence, 31* (121), 35-48.

Hoge, R. D. (1999). *Assessing adolescents in educational, counseling, and other settings.* London: Lawrence Erlbaum Associates, Publishers.

Jackson, A., & Davis, G. (2000). *Turning points 2000: Educating adolescents in the 21st century.* New York: Teachers College Press.

Jarvinen, D. W., & Nicholls, J. G. (1996). Adolescents' social goals, beliefs about causes of social success, and satisfaction in peer relations. *Developmental Psychology, 32,* 435-441.

Johnston, H. J. (with J. Maria de Perez). (1985, January). Four climates of effective middle schools. *Schools in the Middle.* National Association of Secondary School Principals.

Josselson, R. (1994). The theory of identity development and the question of intervention: An introduction. In Sally L. Archer (Ed.), *Interventions for adolescent identity development* (pp.12-28). London: Sage.

Journal of American Medical Association. (2000, May). Retrieved May 2000 from the World Wide Web: http:/jama.ama-assn,org/

Kinney, P., Munroe, M., & Sessions, P. (2000). *A school-wide approach to student-led conferences: A practitioner's guide.* Westerville, OH: National Middle School Association.

Kostanski, M., & Gullune, E. (1998). Adolescent body image dissatisfaction: Relationships with self-esteem, anxiety, and depression controlling for body mass. *Journal of Child Psychology/Psyschiatry, 39,* 255-262.

Larson, R., Richards, M., Meneta, G., & Duckett, E. (1996). Changes in adolescents' daily interactions with their families from age 10-18: Disengagement and transformation. *Developmental Psychology, 32,* 744-754.

L'Esperance, M.E. (1997). *How do we take interdiscipinary teaming to the next level?* Raleigh, NC: North Carolina Middle School Association.

Magen, Z. (1998). *Exploring adolescent happiness: Commitment, purpose, and fulfillment.* London: Sage.

McLean, C. (1998, November 16) Growing up too soon. *Alberta Report/Newsmagazine, 25* (48). 39-41.

Milgram, J. (1992) A portrait of diversity: The middle level student. In Judith L. Irvin(Ed.), *Transforming middle level education: Perspectives and possibilities* (pp. 16-27). Boston: Allyn and Bacon.

National Center for Chronic Disease Prevention and Health Promotion. (1999). Guidelines for school health programs to promote healthy eating. Retrieved April 2001 from the World Wide Web: http://www.cdc.gov/nccdphp/dash/

National Middle School Association. (1982). *This we believe.* Columbus, OH: Author.

National Middle School Association. (1992). *This we believe.* Columbus, OH: Author.

National Middle School Association. (1995). *This we believe: Developmentally responsive middle level schools.* Columbus, OH: Author.

Newcomb, M.D. (1996). Adolescence: Pathologizing a normal process. *Counseling Psychologist, 24,* 482-491.

O'Dea, J., & Abraham, S. (1999). Onset of disordered eating attitudes and behaviors in early adolescence: Interplay of pubertal status, gender, weight, and age. *Adolescence, 34,* 671-679.

Papini, D.R. (1994). Family interventions. In S. L Archer (Ed.), *Interventions for adolescent identity development* (pp.47-61). London: Sage.

Piaget, J. (1970) *Science of education and the psychology of the child.* New York: Penguin Books.

Piaget, J. (1972). Intellectual evolution from adolescence to adulthood. *Human Development, 15,* 1-12.

Pinkowish, M. D., & Saunders, C. S. (1998). Teen milk intake increases bone mineral acquisition. *Patient Care, 32,* 124.

Purkey, W. W., & Strahan, D. B. (1986). *Positive discipline: A pocketful of ideas.* Columbus, OH: National Middle School Association.

Roesser, R. W., Eccles, J. S., & Sameroff, A. J. (2000). School as a context of early adolescents' academic and social-emotional development: A summary of research findings. The Elementary School Journal, 100 (5), 454-471.

Scales, P. C. (1996). A responsive ecology for positive young adolescent development. *Clearing House, 69,* 226-230.

Scales, P. C. (1999). Increasing service-learning's impact on middle school students. *Middle School Journal, 30* (5), 40-44.

Scaramella, L. V., Conger, R. D., Simons, R. L., & Whitebeck, L. B. (1998). Predicting risk for pregnancy by late adolescence: A social contextual perspective. *Developmental Psychology, 34,* 1233-1248.

Smart, M. S., & Smart, R. C. (1973). *Adolescence.* New York: Macmillan Publishing Co.

Stevenson, C. (1998). *Teaching ten to fourteen year olds* (2nd ed.). New York: Longman.

Strahan, D. B. (1985). Frames of mind: A broader view of intellectual development in the middle grades. *Journal of North Carolina League of Middle/Junior High Schools,* 8-10.

Strahan, D. B. (1986). Guided thinking: A strategy for transcending seatwork in the middle school. *NASSP Bulletin, 70,* 75-80.

Strahan, D. B. (1989). Disconnected and disruptive students: Who they are, why they behave as they do, and what we can do about it. *Middle School Journal, 21* (2), 1-5.

Strahan, D. B. (1997). *Mindful learning: Teaching self-discipline and academic achievement.* Durham, NC: Carolina Academic Press.

Strahan, D. B., & Strahan, J. (1988). *Revitalizing remediation in the middle grades: An invitational approach.* Reston, VA: National Association of Secondary School Principals.

Strahan, D. B., & Toepfer, C. (1984). Transescent thinking: Renewed rationale for exploratory learning. *Middle School Journal, 15* (2), 8-11.

Thinklab. (1974). Chicago: Science Research Associates.

Van Hoose, J. (1983). Television: A major cause of undesirable behavior. *NASSP Bulletin 67* (463), 97-101.

Van Hoose, J. (1989). An at-risk program that works. *Middle School Journal, 21* (2), 6-8.

Van Hoose, J. (1991). The ultimate goal: A/A across the day. *Midpoints, 2* (1). Columbus, OH: National Middle School Association.

Van Hoose, J., & Legrand, P. (2000). It takes parents, the whole village, and school to raise the children. *Middle School Journal, 31* (3), 32-37.

Woolfolk, A. E. (1998). *Educational psychology.* (7th Ed.), Boston: Allyn and Bacon.

Zimmerman, M., Copeland, L.A., Shope, J. T., & Dielman, T.E. (1997). A longitudinal study of self-esteem: Implications for adolescent development. *Journal of Youth and Adolescence, 26,* 117-141.